Easy
Hand
Tricks

Bob Longe

Sterling Publishing Co., Inc.
New York

Library of Congress Cataloging-in-Publication Data

Longe, Bob, 1928–
    Easy hand tricks / Bob Longe.
        p.   cm.
    Includes index.
    Summary: Instructions for over 100 tricks that can be performed using only your hands.
    ISBN 1-4027-0779-7
    1. Magic tricks—Juvenile literature. [1. Magic tricks.] I. Title.
GV1548.L565   2004
793.8--dc22

                        2003017491

10 9 8 7 6 5 4 3 2

Published by Sterling Publishing Co., Inc.
387 Park Avenue South, New York, NY 10016
© 2003 by Bob Longe
Distributed in Canada by Sterling Publishing
c/o Canadian Manda Group, 165 Dufferin Street,
Toronto, Ontario, Canada M6K 3H6
Distributed in Great Britain and Europe by Chris Lloyd at Orca Book
Services, Stanley House, Fleets Lane, Poole BH15 3AJ, England
Distributed in Australia by Capricorn Link (Australia) Pty. Ltd.
P.O. Box 704, Windsor, NSW 2756, Australia

Sterling ISBN 1-4027-0779-7

For information about custom editions, special sales, premium and
corporate purchases, please contact Sterling Special Sales
Department at 800-805-5489 or specialsales@sterlingpub.com.

Contents

INTRODUCTION 7
KIND OF MAGICAL 9
   The "Dig-It" Digit 10
   Thumb Stretch 1 12
   Thumb Stretch 2 14
   Finger Stretch 1 15
   Finger Stretch 2 16
   Confidentially, It Shrinks 18
   Floppy Fingers 19
   The "Broken" Finger 20
   'Round and 'Round She Goes 21
   Impossible Revolution 22
   Come and Go 23
   I Want to Be Hoppy 25
   Magnetic Spoon 1 26
   Magnetic Spoon 2 27
   Rubbery Pencil 29
   Spoiled Spoon 29
   Mentalic 31
   Spooky Spoon 31
   The Loose Thumb 34
FUNNY FINGERS 35
   Listen! 36
   I Said, "Listen!" 36
   Now *Really* Listen! 37
   Are You Still Listening? 38
   Bad Habit 38
   Tough Guess 39

The Farewell Finger 39
The Funny Farewell Finger 39
Eye Test 40
Thumb to Nose 40
A Kiss on the Hand 41
Hot Stuff 42
Hand-Fed 43
Wrong Number 43
The Magic Touch 44
Death Wish 44
Stand on Your Own Two Hands 44
The Trained Flea 45
Pulling the Rug Out 46
That's Show Biz! 47
HANKY PANKY 49
How Silly Can You Get? 50
I'm Just Wild About Hair 51
Tie Game 53
The Mystic Thumb 54
Arrow Dynamic 54
A Soft Frisbee 55
Love Knot 55
The Utility Handkerchief 56
Silly Bill 59
Money Talks 62
Penny Move 63
SOMEWHAT HYPNOTIC 65
We Will Join Together 67
He Has No Pull 67
He Exercises Weakly 68
Using Your Head 69
Just a Touch 70
Strong Arm 70
For Shame! 71
Going Up! 73
Still Going Up! 73
Crank It Up 74
Strong Will 75

Stick 'Em Up. 75
A Real Side-Kick. 76
WANNA BET? 77
Knock It Down 78
Hippety Hop 78
Ahem. 79
A Dollar Down 79
A Hand-Me-Down. 80
How Touching 81
Give It Some Thought 81
Give It *More* Thought 82
Give It *Lots* of Thought 82
The Coin Clutch 82
Hey, Don't Push! 83
He Just Can't Wait. 83
The Dramatic Duo. 84
IMPRESSIONS 85
Beat That Egg 86
That's a Lot of Tap Shoes. 86
Walk a Little Slower 86
The Crawl of the Wild. 86
Poor Little Plane 87
Very Sharp. 87
Squeaky Clean. 87
The More, the Merrier. 88
Little Things Mean a Lot 88
The Animal in Us 88
I Salute You 89
A Little Push 89
Fore . . . Heaven's Sake 90
Number, Please 90
TAKE A GUESS. 91
Excuse Me! 92
Ride Down?. 92
Mirror, Mirror 92
Come Fly with Me. 92
PRESENT ARMS 93
Put On Your Coat. 94

Relax and Unwind. 94
A Good Choke. 95
A Good Backup. 96
Double-Jointed. 96
SHOWTIME. 97
A Pat on the Head 98
It's Superman!. 99
Mime Time 1 99
Mime Time 2 100
Mime Time 3 101
Mime Time 4 103
A Touching Experience 104
Creepy Caterpillar 105
And the Beat Goes On. 106
Finger Folly 106
And One Left Over 107
Miraculous Multiplication 107
Snatch and Grab It. 109
Dead Digit 110
MANEUVERS 111
Greetings Gate, Let's Coordinate. 112
Climbing Up!. 112
Honk, Honk. 113
I Got Rhythm 114
Finger Wiggle 115
Let's Coordinate. 115
Tough Workout 116
MAGICAL FEET. 117
Take a Walk 118
But Seriously, Folks 118
Take a Stand 118
Dancing Fool 119
It's Underfoot 119
Towel Trick 1 120
Towel Trick 2 120
Towel Trick 3 121
The Big Jump 121
MASTERY LEVELS CHART & INDEX 123

Introduction

Imagine! Here are 129 clever tricks you can perform anywhere, anytime. How can this be? Simple. The only equipment you need is your own hands. Oh, yes, I threw in several tricks with the feet. And a handkerchief. And your mouth. And some common household objects.

It's true: You can perform all sorts of magic tricks using hands and feet, and nothing else—not even manipulative skill. With the information provided here, you can amuse yourself and others with a few tricks or with an entire routine.

You can stretch your fingers or thumbs and perform dozens of other cute "quickies" just using your fingers. With hands and feet you can perform all sorts of hilarious imitations.

How about some tricks using your arms? Why not? If there's one thing that's connected to an arm, it's a hand.

And there are many stunts, impressions, and maneuvers featuring the hands.

To top things off, you're provided with several amusing challenges: You can do them; the spectators can't.

Kind
of
Magical

Clearly, no trick is more readily available than one using only the hands.

The "Dig-It" Digit

Apparently, you remove a finger. This is always quite amusing, especially for children. Everyone, including children, *knows* that you didn't actually remove the digit. But just *maybe* you somehow were able to do it. Here you evidently remove the first finger of your right hand. This is undoubtedly the oldest, and best known, of this type of trick. Here you discover how to do it absolutely correctly.

Begin by making this announcement: "I have some amazing feats for you. Actually, they're not feats, but hands. Just watch these magical fingers."

Wiggle your fingers, demonstrating their amazing flexibility. Move your left hand so that the fingers are pointing down and the back of the hand is toward the spectators.

Tuck your left thumb into your left palm. The left hand now goes in front of the right hand. When the left hand conceals the right fingers, bend in the first finger of the right hand. Rest the left palm on the back of the right hand, fingers still pointing down. (The broken outline in Illus. 1 shows the position of the left hand.)

 Illus. 1

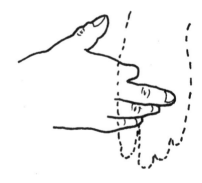

"Watch, and you'll see something truly amazing."

Twist the left hand upward, raising the second, third, and fourth fingers as a unit. The first finger stays down, hiding the fact that your left thumb is bent inward. The illusion is that your left thumb is the outer joint of your right first finger (Illus. 2).

Slide the left thumb along the surface of the right second finger several times, demonstrating that the outer joint of the right first finger is separated from the rest of the finger (Illus. 3).

Extend the left fingers downward again and straighten out the right first finger, grasping it in the left hand. Twist your left hand around the finger several times.

"I'm just repairing the finger. It should be all right in a minute."

Hold the right first finger up and waggle it, showing that it is fully restored.

Illus. 2

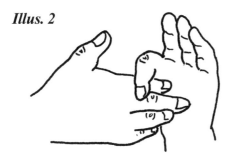

Illus. 3

Thumb Stretch 1

Detaching a digit is always droll, of course, but there are many other hand tricks available—stretching a digit, for instance. Here we have a very easy way to stretch your thumb. Apparently.

Form your right hand into a fist with the thumb sticking out on top (Illus. 4). Let everyone get a good look.

Illus. 4

"This is a really remarkable thumb," you declare.

Place the right hand into the left, so that the right thumb is gripped by the left thumb. Illus. 5 gives your view. The upper part of the right thumb should stick out far enough to be seen by the group.

Illus. 5

"Before your very eyes, I'm going to stretch my thumb. I don't need to tell you that this is going to be *extremely* difficult. In fact, I'll have to hold the thumb with my teeth."

Tilt both hands back to your mouth. The audience should no longer be able to see your thumb. Move your right thumb down and push your left thumb up.

Close your teeth over the end of your left thumb. If you've been sufficiently smooth with your transition, the group should assume that you've bitten into your *right* thumb. The left thumb should be held up as straight as possible; thus, it could pass as *either* thumb. The circumstances, however, make it seem to be the right thumb.

Illus. 6

Bend your head forward, still retaining the grip of your teeth on the thumb. It really looks as though you're holding the right thumb between your teeth.

Now you slowly *pull* the right hand downward several inches (Illus. 6). Be sure to move it far enough so that people can see that you're not merely moving the rest of the hand away from the thumb. (The left hand, of course, masks the true picture.) While making this move, you should appear to be straining.

Pause long enough so that all can see what you've done. But don't linger for too long. Several seconds should be plenty.

Slide your right hand upward and, at the same time, move your head back up. No one should be able to see your thumb. Remove the left thumb from your mouth. Raise up your right hand, bringing it through the left hand.

Let your left hand drop as you stare at your right hand. Waggle it a bit. Shake your head, saying, "Now how am I going to get those teeth marks out?"

Thumb Stretch 2

Years ago I read a complicated method of accomplishing the thumb stretch *without* using the teeth. When I tried it out, I discovered that it was difficult to do with my short fingers. So I adapted the stunt to my stubby little hand. *This* version—quite different from the one I came across—can be done by anyone.

"Of course I'm able to stretch my right thumb," you announce. "After all, I'm right-handed. But can I stretch my *left* thumb? We're about to find out."

Display your thumb precisely as described at the beginning of the previous trick—that is, form your hand into a fist with the thumb sticking out on top. The only difference is that you display your *left* thumb.

Grasp the left thumb with your right first two fingers on the audience side and your right thumb on your side. The right thumb should be directly behind the left and pointing, up precisely as the left thumb is. The only difference is that the right thumb is about an inch below the left.

Slide your right two fingers and thumb upward until the left thumb is hidden. At this point, extend your right thumb upward. If the timing is right, it will seem to the group that they're still seeing the left thumb grasped by your first two right fingers.

Continue sliding the right hand upward at least a few inches. As you do so, be sure to grimace as though in pain and perhaps groan a bit. Exactly how far should you slide your right hand upward? I slide until my right second finger covers the fingernail of the left thumb. Your best bet is to check it out in the mirror and see what works for you.

Don't leave the thumb extended for more than a few seconds. Then reverse the moves. When you're back to gripping the left thumb with the first two fingers of the right hand, twist these fingers back and forth, as though massaging that poor sore digit.

"That smarts," you declare. Separate the hands and display the left thumb.

Your practice in front of a mirror will be well rewarded, for this is probably the most effective of all the digit-stretching tricks.

Finger Stretch 1

Here we have a combination of optical illusion and subtle trickery.

Hold up the first finger of your left hand, declaring, "I am going to make every effort to stretch this finger. But don't expect miracles; it may stretch out only an inch or two."

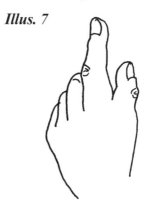

Illus. 7

Place the finger on your right leg, with the other fingers folded at the second joint. Have it bent up somewhat (Illus. 7). Put your right first finger on top crosswise. It should be a bit below the fingernail of the left first finger (Illus. 8).

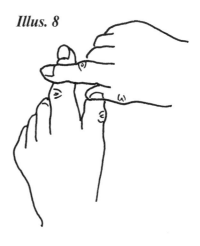

Illus. 8

Move your right first finger rapidly back and forth along the left first finger, from the bottom portion of the fingernail to the second joint (Illus. 9). As you do so, gradually push down on the left first finger so that it extends to its maximum length. This must be done over a period of at least ten seconds.

Illus. 9

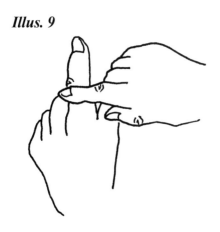

Also, and this is of great importance, as you push the first finger out, bring the visible portions of the other three fingers back and under. Originally, the fingers were folded at the second joint. Now they are bent completely under the hand. Compare the illustrations to see what I mean.

Three things happen: (1) The back-and-forth motion creates an illusion of the finger lengthening; (2) The extension of the finger to its maximum length actually makes it longer; (3) Folding the other fingers completely beneath the hand creates the illusion that the first finger has gotten longer.

As you smoothly combine the elements, it may even seem to you that the finger is growing longer.

Finger Stretch 2

In the description of this trick, it may seem to you that the fingers must be contorted. *Not so!* I couldn't possibly perform a trick that would call for unusual stretches of the fingers. But I can do this trick perfectly. And so can you. Give it a try.

Implied in all descriptions of this trick is that the positioning of the fingers must be done in advance, with no witnesses. I've devised a wrinkle that enables you to proceed with everyone watching.

If you're doing a routine, you might begin like this: "You've just seen me stretch out the first finger on my *left* hand. Let's see if I can do an even better job with the first finger on my *right* hand."

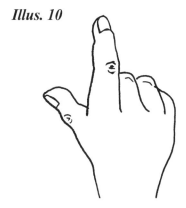

Illus. 10

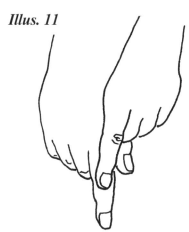

Illus. 11

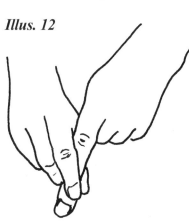

Illus. 12

Otherwise, you can begin with a comment like this: "When the weather is just right, I can actually stretch my first finger. Watch!"

As you speak, display the first finger of your right hand and waggle it (Illus. 10). Bend over till you're almost at a right angle. Bring your hands in to your stomach so that no one can see what you're up to.

And here's what you *are* up to: Put your right first finger on top of your left first finger so that it covers the second joint (Illus. 11). Now put your left second finger over the right first finger so that the first finger's nail is covered (Illus. 12). (Try this out. Now go to a mirror and take a look. Pretty good, eh?)

As you do the preceding move, grunt as though in pain. "That *hurts* when I stretch it. Maybe I stretched it too far. What do you think?"

Straighten up, leaving your hands at waist level. Display your stretched finger. Let everyone get a good look.

To finish, just ram your right first finger between the

Illus. 13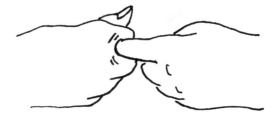

first and second fingers of your left hand (Illus. 13). Twist your fingers around it for a bit. Then pull it out and hold it up. Exhale in relief.

"Ah, that's better."

Confidentially, It Shrinks

Not only can you remove a finger, you can also shrink one.

Hold your left hand up straight, its back to the onlookers. Grip the little finger of the left hand with your right hand. The first finger and thumb of the right hand hold the top knuckle. The remaining fingers of the right hand are cupped outward (Illus. 14).

Illus. 14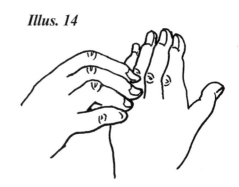

Push downward with the right thumb and first finger, holding the top of the finger straight. At the same time, however, you are bending the lower knuckle of the little finger outward. You are concealing this bend with the second, third, and fourth right fingers.

Very slowly, you push the little finger down, laboriously reducing its size. The illusion is quite realistic, since the tip of the finger remains pointing upward, and the finger is sliding down next to straight, extended fingers (Illus. 15).

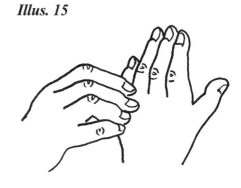

Illus. 15

Agonize as you pull the finger back up. Repeat the reduction. You might even try it a third time. Finally, pull the finger back up, grasp it with the right hand, and rub it vigorously. Then show the left hand, moving all the fingers to show that everything is as it should be.

Floppy Fingers

"Perhaps you've noticed how good I am at stretching things: fingers, thumbs, the truth. You name it, I'll stretch it. If you've wondered how I'm able to do such fabulous tricks with my digits, I'll be happy to explain."

As you make this last statement, hold up your hands and wiggle your fingers.

"The fact is, I happen to be extremely lucky. You see, I have rubber fingers. Watch!"

Hold your hands together in a praying position. The following actions are performed very rapidly. Leaning the hands slightly to your left, move the right hand up over the left, wrapping the right fingers over the left fingers.

Then, leaning the hands slightly to the right, move the left hand up over the right, wrapping the left fingers over the right fingers. Continue alternating this move rapidly and without stopping. Do this at least six times on each side. (I mentally count to 12, adding one for each time I make the basic move.)

Try this in front of a mirror. The illusion is that your fingers are indeed extraordinarily rubbery.

The "Broken" Finger

You appear to break off a finger and then restore it. Ken de Courcy invented this very clever method.

The digit you're going to break off is your left middle finger. Start with your left hand held up palm upward, with the fingers spread wide apart and pointing up.

With the right hand, approach the left from above, fingers pointing down. The right fingers should be cupped, almost claw-like. When the right hand obscures the audience's view of the left middle finger, bend it back so that the tip almost rests in the left palm. (Make sure that the right thumb is held back to clear the way for the left middle finger.)

Apparently grip the top portion of the left middle finger with the clawlike right fingers in front and the thumb in back. The left fingers on either side are spread out so that the audience has a good view of the grip.

With a sudden sharp movement, bend the right hand forward, as though breaking off the middle finger. At the same time, make a loud cracking noise with your mouth.

Hold your right hand up, back to the audience, apparently holding the detached digit. Hold the left hand fairly close to the body so that no one can get a side view.

"It's easy enough for a lunatic to break off one of his fingers," you explain, "but it takes a crazy magician to restore it."

Bring the right hand over the left as before and apparently put the finger back on the left hand. Naturally, when the right hand covers the opening left by the missing finger, you straighten out that finger. (Make sure the right thumb is held back and out of the way to allow clearance for the left middle finger.) The concluding movement is to slide your right hand upward and off the restored finger.

'Round and 'Round She Goes

This brief, extraordinary stunt is a real reputation maker. Apparently, you are either a magician or double-jointed, for you can turn your hand completely around in a manner that is physically impossible.

To start, you must be wearing a suit jacket or sport coat, or the equivalent. For example, a sweater with long, loose sleeves will do. Now you are going to kneel down, press your hand against the floor, and turn it 360 degrees. It will seem quite impossible, and will look ridiculous. When people see you do it, they will either laugh or gasp.

The secret is quite simple, however, and you will accomplish the feat easily on your first try. "Ladies and gentlemen," you might say, "I have been practicing magic for some time. As a result, I have gained astonishing control over various parts of my body. Let me show you."

Illus. 16

Kneel down. Grasp your right sleeve with your left hand so that you can hold it in place while performing your maneuver. Turn your right hand palm-up and twist that hand counterclockwise as far as you can. Rest the *back of your right hand* on the floor (Illus. 16). You should be feeling some strain in your arm and wrist, but it will be quite brief, for you will begin the maneuver immediately. Very slowly rotate your right arm clockwise, holding the sleeve so that it stays steady. Your hand, still

pressed against the floor, also turns clockwise, of course. You strain a bit at the end to bring the hand to precisely the position it was in at the beginning. Illus. 17 shows the hand at various phases of the move.

Leave the hand in its final position for a few seconds and then stand up, shaking your hand and arm.

"How did you do that?" people will ask. Don't tell them. If you do, you will turn an astonishing feat into an insignificant little trick. And for heaven's sake, don't repeat it—at least on that occasion. Retrospectively, spectators assume that you performed the stunt with your hand palm down; don't shatter that illusion. The secret is not well known, so let's keep it that way.

Impossible Revolution

When it comes to revolving your hand in a complete circle, the method I just described is really good. But here is a method that is more challenging and also more astonishing. For some, this stunt might prove too severe a strain. So if the starting position seems too difficult, *don't* bother with the trick. Stick to the previous method, which is much easier.

To perform this, you need to revolve your hand on a table. If you're extremely nimble, you could accomplish the same effect on the floor. I am not, so I need to do it at a table.

What's the difference between working on a table or on the floor? On the floor, you have a very difficult time maneuvering your body. That's right. Moving the entire body is an important part of the effect.

Let me describe the method in detail.

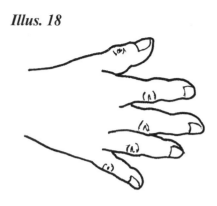

Stand with your right side toward the table. Place your right hand palm-down on the table, with the little finger nearest your body. In other words, the hand is severely twisted counterclockwise. The hand is almost parallel with the side of the table (Illus. 18). *Bend your elbow.* Turn your hand even further counterclockwise. Twist it until it hurts a little. (It will hurt only briefly because, as before, you'll start the movement almost immediately.)

Start turning the hand clockwise. Do this fairly slowly. As you do so, gradually turn your body as well, so that at the conclusion of the movement you are facing the table. Force your hand to move clockwise as far as possible. Strain a little. Your hand should be back to its original position (or darned close to it).

Stop. You're done.

Note

The real secret to this stunt is body position. Yes, you have to strain somewhat at both ends of the twist, but the body movement guarantees a much bigger circle.

Come and Go

This ancient trick appeared in my book *Easy Magic Tricks*. It might be old, but it's still effective, *and* amusing.

Some may remember this stunt from their childhood. No matter. It is amusing to those who have seen it before, and amazing to those who haven't.

You should be seated at a table. Tear off two bits of paper

from a napkin, a tissue, or a paper towel. Moisten them and stick one on the fingernail of each first finger.

Place the tips of your first fingers on the edge of the table. Bouncing the two fingers rhythmically, you chant line one: "Two little birds sitting on a hill . . ."

Bounce the right finger as you say, "One called Jack . . ."

Bounce the left finger as you say, "And one called Jill."

"Go away, Jack." As you say this, swing your right hand up and past your head. During the swing up, you fold in your first finger and extend your second finger. Instantly bring the hand down to the table, displaying the second finger.

Immediately say, "Go away, Jill." Perform the same switching action with the left hand. No one has time to observe what you actually did, because you proceed without hesitation to the next step.

Swing the right hand up again and switch fingers again as you say, "Come back, Jack." Instantly do the same with the left hand, saying, "Come back, Jill."

The key is to perform the stunt *rapidly*. Once you start, the whole sequence should last no more than ten seconds. A few minutes' practice should give you complete mastery.

Here's the ditty in one chunk:

"Two little birds sitting on a hill,
One called Jack, one called Jill.
Go away, Jack. Go away, Jill.
Come back, Jack. Come back, Jill."

Note

As time has passed, I've realized that there's much more that can be done with this basic idea. For instance, you can make both birds fly away at once. Change the rhyme to:

"Go away Jack and also Jill.
Come back Jack and also Jill."

You can also make the bird fly from one hand to the other. First show the bird on the right hand and nothing on the left.

Then, show that the bird has left the right hand and gone to the left. The rhyme could be:

"One little bird sitting on a hill,

Jumps on over for he can't sit still."

The key, as before, is to perform rapidly. Don't give spectators a chance to notice which fingers are actually being used.

I Want to Be Hoppy

Since the principle here is the same as that of Come and Go, you should avoid doing both tricks for the same group at the same time.

The original version of this stunt called for a cigar band. I seldom know where to find one, so I usually use one of these: a colored rubber band wound around the finger several times; an address label, moistened and attached to the finger; a scrap of thin paper (such as a napkin or tissue), moistened and stuck on the finger; or a plastic bandage.

Which finger? The second finger of the right hand. Let us assume you have wound a colored plastic bandage around your second finger. Extend the first two fingers of the right hand. Make sure that the other fingers are well folded in and the thumb is out of sight (Illus. 19).

Illus. 19

Hold out the left hand palm up; the right hand should be about eight inches above the left. Bring the right hand down to the left hand, displaying briefly the extended two fingers of the right

Illus. 20

hand. Leave the fingers there for only a fraction of a second—just long enough for onlookers to see them; then bring the right hand up to its original position. As you bring the right hand down again to display the fingers, fold in the first finger and extend the third finger (Illus. 20).

"Watch it hop!" you say. Bring the right hand up again. Then, as you bring it down, switch fingers once more. Repeat the switch several times, *rapidly*. The illusion is that the colored plastic bandage is hopping back and forth between the fingers.

Magnetic Spoon 1

This classic stunt is a perfect introduction to Magnetic Spoon 2. Ancient it might be, but this golden oldie still provides oodles of fun.

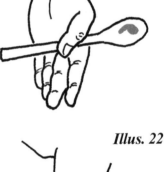

Illus. 21

Hold a tablespoon on your left palm with your left thumb (Illus. 21). Grip your left wrist with your right hand. Turn the left hand over, revolving it in the right hand, which remains still. As you do this, turn the hand downward so that the left fingers point toward the floor. At the same time, extend your right first finger so that it holds the spoon. Now stick your left thumb out so that all can see it (Illus. 22).

Illus. 22

Move the hands together back and forth. The spoon mysteriously clings to the palm of your left hand. Stop the movement and then precisely reverse the steps you performed in turning the left hand over. First, bring the left thumb in onto the spoon. Then turn the left hand palm up as you return the right first finger to the side of the wrist.

You may repeat the trick if you wish. And, since the trick is so well known anyway, you might even teach it to interested spectators. The next spoon suspension, however, you will *not* teach; it is much too good a trick.

Magnetic Spoon 2

Magic! Comedy! Surprise! What's more, a neat little "sucker" effect.

Hold up a tablespoon and say, "I will now glue this to the palm of my hand." You attach it to your hands by interlocking your fingers so that the second finger of the left hand actually slides into the palm of the right hand while the remaining fingers interlock alternately. Illus. 23 shows the positions as seen from the front and from the rear. As you interlock the fingers, slide the

Illus. 23

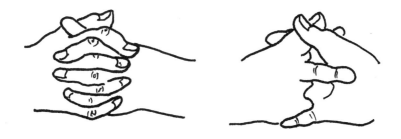

spoon under the left second finger so that it is held secure against the right palm (Illus. 24). Naturally, you do not perform this procedure in plain sight. If sitting at a table, take the spoon under the table and attach it to the hands. If standing up, simply turn away

for a moment while per-
forming the dirty work.

Bring the hands and
spoon into sight, with
backs of the hands toward
spectators and spoon per-
pendicular to the floor.
Hold the thumbs down in
your palms so that
onlookers get the impres-
sion that the thumbs are
holding the spoon. Move
the hands from side to
side. "See? The spoon is glued on."

If no one comments about your thumbs, say, "You seem
skeptical. The thumbs? Not at all." Raise your right thumb above
your hand. "See? One thumb." Lower the right thumb and raise
the left thumb. "And there's the other thumb."

Move the hands from side to side with the left thumb raised.
If no one raises an objection, pretend to hear one. "Both thumbs?
Oh, all right!"

Raise the other thumb. What! The thumbs aren't holding the
spoon? But how . . .?

Wave your hands about, moving them backward and forward,
side to side. Even tilt the hands, bringing them almost level, making sure no one can see that sneaky second finger which is gripping the spoon.

Abruptly separate the hands, taking the spoon in one. Set it
down and show both sides of your hands. No stickum, no rubber
bands—just sheer magic. As we have suspected all along, you are
a witch.

The stunt may also be performed with a pencil, but I find it
a little harder on my second finger.

Rubbery Pencil

Endear yourself to your hostess by demonstrating that she's buffoon enough to keep a rubber pencil in the house. Just pick up one of her pencils and proceed.

Illus. 25

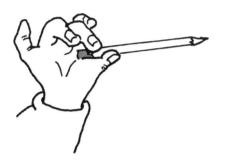

Hold the pencil *loosely* near the end between the second finger on top and the thumb on the bottom (Illus. 25). Rapidly and repeatedly move your hand up and down about a half inch or so. The pencil will be making a countermovement of about two inches or so. When you have the rhythm just right, the illusion is that the pencil is bending as you wave it.

Practice in front of a mirror until even you are deceived.

As you perform the stunt, you might explain to your hostess, "I can't believe you're such a practical joker . . . keeping a rubber pencil around."

Spoiled Spoon

A good follow-up to Rubbery Pencil is this somewhat more challenging stunt.

Apparently you bend a spoon; actually, you are merely sneaky. You will have to practice this one a bit, but it is well worth it, especially when you consider how many people you can irritate.

At the table, you might begin by picking up a spoon and commenting, "My, this looks like strong silverware. Let me check."

Now you perform your infamous bending routine. Hold the spoon in the right hand as in Illus. 26. Note that your hand is fairly high on the handle, with the thumb above it. Rest the bowl of the spoon on the table, and place your left hand on the right (Illus. 27). With an apparent effort, you make a forward movement as though bending the handle up at a right angle. Actually, the handle remains straight. Your right third and fourth fingers retain their grip beneath the handle as the rest of the hand moves forward. Take away the left hand. The spoon is now supported by the third and fourth fingers beneath (Illus. 28).

"Pretty strong," you comment as you lift the "bent" spoon off the table. Immediately toss it down, showing that it is actually not bent at all. If you are a guest, you certainly do not want your hostess to have a coronary.

Illus. 26

Illus. 27

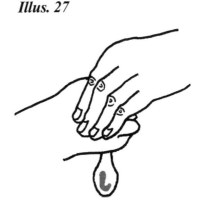

Illus. 28

Mentalic

Let's turn to a few effects that require no manual manipulation.

For an astonishing mental effect, you will require a stooge, or—as magicians prefer—a confederate. In advance, tell Susie that you'd like her to assist you. Then explain:

"I'll get you and someone else to participate in an attempt at mentalism. I will close my eyes. Each of you will hold up a number of fingers from one to five. I'll ask what the total is. One of you will tell me. Then I'll say what number each of you is holding up.

"The reason I'll know, Susie, is that you start by holding up three fingers. So I just subtract that from the total and I have both numbers. The next time, you hold up the same number of fingers that the other person held up before. So, you hold up three fingers the first time, and the other person holds up four. Someone tells me that the total is seven. I say, 'Three and four.' The next time, you hold up *four* fingers, the same number the other person had. And, from then on, you hold up the previous number held by the other person."

Perform the stunt at least three or four times. Assuming Susie does it right, and you know how to subtract, the trick should go over extremely well.

Spooky Spoon

Have I ever lied to you? Not that you remember, right? Well, please believe me on this: If you don't try another trick in this book, try this one. It's absolutely eerie!

Years ago you could use a certain kind of skeleton key to accomplish a similar effect, but I don't believe that the effect is nearly as strong as that obtained with a tablespoon.

To check out how it works, place a tablespoon on your extended fingers, with the humped side of the bowl *up*, as in

Illus. 29. Note that the bowl is *off* the hand. The spoon may want to turn over immediately. This means that you must tip the hand down slightly. With a bit of trial and error, you'll discover exactly the point at which the spoon will lie there stable.

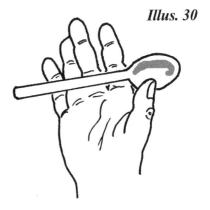

Illus. 29

Illus. 30

Wave your other hand over the spoon. As you do so, gradually and imperceptibly tip your hand up. With a minimum of movement—practically none, in fact—the spoon will roll over toward you (Illus. 30). The first few times, and maybe all the time, it will look magical *to you*. Imagine the effect on an audience.

How do you use this marvelous trick? You can tell this kind of story: "A certain tribe of Indians (your choice) used eating implements to tell the future. I've found that we can accomplish the same thing with a certain kind of tablespoon, providing we make the proper mystical waves over it." Or, " . . . providing we say the magical Indian words."

Place the spoon on your hand. Say to Ellen, "Please ask the spoon a question. If the answer is no, the spoon will stay as it is. If the answer is yes, the spoon may move slightly."

Note how you underplay the movement of the spoon. When it eventually answers yes, you'll hear oohs and ahhs.

Ellen asks a question. Depending on your mood, you have the spoon answer yes or no. Do this a few more times, making sure there are at least a few yes answers.

Quit while they're still amazed.

Notes

(1) If someone says that the spoon made an incorrect answer, say, "I said that the spoon would answer your questions; I *didn't* say that the spoon was particularly intelligent."

(2) You'll probably find this out for yourself soon enough, but *don't try to make the spoon roll back.* After it has rolled over, pick it up, turn it over, and replace it on your hand with the humped side of the bowl up.

(3) It is best to try to prevent others from experimenting with the trick. Obviously, you can't prevent this if other tablespoons are lying about. But you can at least put *your* spoon away. It will help also if you distract the group by immediately moving on to another stunt.

(4) When performing for children, I frequently do an amusing stunt with a handkerchief. It can be done equally well with the rolling spoon. Place the spoon on your hand and talk about its mystical powers. "In fact, the spoon seems to know that someone in this room is very silly. And when I wave my hand over it and say the magic words, the spoon will roll over *toward* that silly person. All I have to do . . ."

As you continue speaking, the spoon rolls over in *your* direction. But, despite the giggles and laughter, you don't notice for a while. Finally, you look down and see what's happened.

A bit flustered, you say, "All right, we'll start in just a minute." Arrange the spoon on your hand again. "As I said, there's a very silly person in this room, and when I wave my hand and say . . ." Unbeknown to you, the spoon rolls in your direction again. You can repeat this a number of times as you get increasingly perturbed and the children laugh harder.

The Loose Thumb

Finally, in this section, let's try a trick with your thumb. This one looks quite realistic, and it has a plot to it.

Hold up your left hand with its back to the audience; fingers are extended toward your right, and the thumb is pointed upward.

"See this thumb? It's most peculiar. Every so often it gets very loose. I think that it gets unscrewed. Right now it works fine, but just let me see if I can unscrew it for you."

What's required for this trick is your ability to act. And please don't give in to the temptation of trying to be funny; the value of the stunt lies in your totally serious demeanor.

With your right hand, grip the left thumb from above, holding it between fingers and thumb. Go through a twisting motion, as though unscrewing the thumb. As you do this, the left hand will probably move somewhat back and forth. This is fine; it adds to the illusion.

"Maybe that's enough."

Make a loose fist with your right hand and wrap it around your thumb. Pull upward. Try harder; your right hand comes free, moving upward.

"No, it has to be twisted a little more."

Go through the twisting procedure a bit more. Again, try to pull up your thumb, without success.

Do the entire bit once more.

Finally, go to grip the thumb with your right hand. As the right hand conceals the thumb, lower the thumb into the palm of the left hand. Tug a few times. Then lift the right hand away from the left three or four inches.

"I got it!"

Maintain the position only briefly. Lower the right hand to the left. Raise the left thumb into the right hand. Move your right hand away, showing that the thumb has returned. As an afterthought, give the thumb several turns in the opposite direction.

"Better tighten it up, so that it doesn't fall off."

Funny Fingers

Magic tricks with the hands are always entertaining—and there are many more coming—but countless other types of hand tricks are available. Most of them are somewhere between amusing and hilarious. Here we have some guaranteed laugh-getters that you can perform between more serious efforts.

Listen!
• • • • • • • •

The next four items could comprise a routine. Randy should be susceptible to this sort of nonsense.

"I'm going to give you an IQ test, Randy. Is that all right?"
Of course.

"Be sure to follow these directions, okay?" Stick up your thumbs as you say, "Raise two fingers."

Chances are he will lift his thumbs.

"Very nice, Randy. But those aren't fingers; they're thumbs."
Pause.

"We'll try again some other time."

I Said, "Listen!"
• • • • • • • • • • • • • • • • • • • •

This is similar to the above. You can do it as a follow-up.

"I'll give you another chance, Randy. You must be aware that people today just can't seem to follow directions. But I'm sure you'll be the exception. We'll try to make some letters with our fingers. Ready?"

With your right hand use your thumb and first finger to form the letter L. (Illus. 31 shows your view.)

"Do you know what this is?"
The letter L.

"Can you make one?"
He does.

"Very good."

Illus. 31

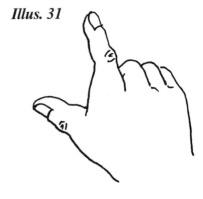

Cross your first fingers, making an X.

"Can you make this?"
He does.

With your right first finger and thumb, form a C, the remaining fingers extended.

"Can you make a C?"

He does. Turn it upside-down.

"Can you do this?"

He does.

"Can you press it on your chin?" As you say this, press it against your cheek.

Randy will probably push it against his cheek.

"Hey, I said *chin*. Please pay attention."

Now *Really* Listen!

Form the letter C, just as you did before, with the remaining fingers extended.

"All right, Randy, do you remember what this is?"

The letter C.

"Right." Bring the tips of the right first finger and thumb together, while keeping the other fingers extended. As you can see, this forms the "okay" sign (Illus. 32). "And what's this?"

Chances are that Randy will have some idea of its meaning. If not, say, "Most people would think that it means that everything is okay."

Regardless, go on, "That's just not true, Randy. Actually, this is *Thursday.*"

Illus. 32

Touch your little finger with your thumb, saying, "This is Monday." Touch your third finger with your thumb, saying, "Tuesday." Touch your second finger with your thumb, saying, "Wednesday." Touch your first finger with your thumb, forming the "okay" sign. "Thursday."

Are You Still Listening?

I believe it's all right to abuse Randy one more time.

Hold up your first finger.

"Why can't the President use this finger, Randy?"

I don't know.

"Because it's mine."

Bad Habit

Here's a little something borrowed from the great comic Red Skelton.

"Presenting, the last of the great gunfighters," you say.

You now do the following routine:

Make your right hand into a gun, thumb raised and first finger extended (Illus. 33).

Pull back your thumb, saying, "Click." Move your hand forward, saying, "Pow." Bring the hand up, pointing at your mouth. Blow with an audible puff, as though eliminating smoke from the business end of the gun.

Repeat: Click, pow, blow.

Do it again.

This time, after you do the clicking action, bring your hand up as though to blow and intead go, "Pow." Hold the hand out and give a pathetic little puff.

"Oh-oh!" Let your head drop to your shoulder, eyes shut.

Illus. 33

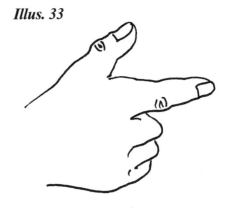

Tough Guess

"I have a question for you."

Hold out your hands, both closed into fists. Move one hand around in every direction while the other remains still.

"Okay. Which hand has the Mexican jumping beans in it?"

The Farewell Finger

You'll need a bread stick for this one. It can't have seeds on it, for it must substitute for a finger.

Bend down the second finger of your left hand. Now a portion of the bread stick goes between the first and third finger, and it's held in place by those digits. See? From a little distance it's a passable finger. And if you limit the hand to gentle motion, it will be completely deceptive.

With your right hand touch the first finger of your left hand, saying, "Let's see, I had breakfast."

Touch the breadstick. "I had lunch."

Touch your third finger. "I had a snack."

Touch your little finger. "I had dinner."

Pause. "Wait a minute. I *didn't* have lunch."

Pull the piece of bread stick from your hand and toss it aside.

The Funny Farewell Finger

Don a glove, but fail to insert the middle finger. Flex the middle finger of the glove with your other hand.

"*What the heck happened to my finger?*"

Finally, pull off the glove. You're happy to note that your finger is still there.

Eye Test

"Time for an eye test, Lucy. All right with you?"

Sure it is.

Rapidly wave two fingers up and down in front of her eyes, saying, "How many, Lucy?"

Naturally, she says two.

While still waving rapidly, you raise a third finger. Stop your hand. Look at it.

"No, Lucy, it's three."

Thumb to Nose

"Rosemary, I'd like you to help me out."

Hold the left hand at nose level, about four inches from your nose. It is palm up and parallel to the floor. The fingers are spread, with the little finger nearest to your face (Illus. 34).

Illus. 34

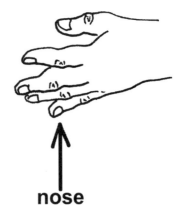

The right hand is spread, palm-down, and parallel to the floor. The right thumb rests on the left little finger, and the right little finger is nearest Rosemary.

"Rosemary, I wonder if you'd pull gradually on my right little finger."

As she does this, your hands gradually pivot around the right thumb and left little finger until the left thumb comes to the nose, with both hands extended out (Illus. 35).

Illus. 35

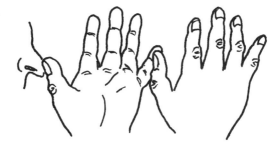

Appear irritated with Rosemary. "Well, gee, Rosemary, I didn't mean for you to pull it like that!"

A Kiss on the Hand

Illus. 36

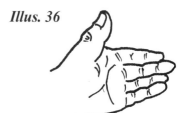

Next, an interesting diversion I invented—in what so many of my friends refer to as my "wasted youth."

You'll need a ballpoint pen. Partially close your left hand so that a wrinkle runs up and down the palm. Draw a short line across the wrinkle (Illus. 36). Draw some protruding lips on either side of the line (Illus. 37).

Illus. 37

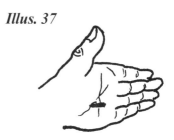

Open up the hand. Draw a male face on the right side of the hand, and a female face on the left (Illus. 38). (Or, if you prefer, vice versa.)

"I would like to provide you with the true story of how a little poem got invented." Show your hand.

Illus. 38

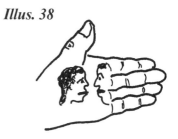

"Jimmy and Jan went together for quite a while. And one day they had a terrible quarrel over which was the worst football team in the National Football League. Just imagine! After they had argued for several hours, Jimmy said, 'Oh, go climb a tree.' And Jan said, '*You* go climb a tree.'

"So they both climbed a tree. Along came Jan's little brother, Herbert, who saw them in the tree. And he began to sing out: 'Jimmy and Jan, sitting in a tree, K-I-S-S-I-N-G.'"

Naturally, as you recite the spelling portion of the ditty, partially close your hand several times, causing Jimmy and Jan to kiss.

"And that is the *true* story of where that little poem came from."

Hot Stuff

"I don't like to brag, but. . . Well, I *do* like to brag; I just seldom have anything to brag about. Anyway, one thing I can brag about is this: I can magically make *any* object super-hot."

Casually show both sides of your hands. "No chemicals in my hands. Will someone please set an object down before me. It can be anything."

It doesn't matter what the object is. It can be anything from a ballpoint pen to a glass of water.

"I only need to make some mystical waves over the object."

Illus. 39

Put your right hand into your pocket as your left hand makes weird waves over the object. Your right hand will find a key and proceed to put a "boo-boo" on your first finger. You do this by putting your first finger under the hole (or one of the holes) of the key as your thumb applies pressure (Illus. 39). After several seconds, you'll have a little lump on your finger that will easily pass for a blister. (Of course, it will disappear very shortly.)

"I think it's hot enough."

Remove your right hand from your pocket. Reach out and touch the object with your first finger. As you touch, make a sudden brief exhalation between your teeth. This will pass for either the sound of pain or the sizzle of heat. It doesn't matter which. Quickly draw your finger back.

"I guess it is hot. Look at the blister." Display your wound.

Wave over the object with your left hand. "It should be cool again."

Touch it again with the same finger. "Yeah, it's all right now."

Hand-Fed

Often a discussion comes up regarding the trouble some people have distinguishing right from left, particularly when driving.

"Easy enough," you might say to Jennifer, who has this problem. "Which hand do you eat with?"

"The right hand," she replies.

"Just wondering. Most people use a fork."

Wrong Number

Illus. 40

Judy once won a spelling bee in the seventh grade, so she'd be the perfect assistant for this stunt.

"Let's try an easy spelling test, Judy. First, we'll arrange your hands."

Have her place her left hand palm down on the table, with the right hand crosswise on top (Illus. 40).

You say, "Now what does this spell: W-I-N-G?"

"Wing."

"Say it three times please."

"Wing, wing, wing."

Pick up her right hand and hold it to your ear, as though answering the phone. In your best Elmer Fudd voice, say, "Hewwo?"

The Magic Touch

This works best if someone, like Ted, has bragged about his ability to touch his nose with his tongue. If you are determined to perform this stunt, though, you can bring up the subject yourself: "Can anyone here touch his nose with his tongue?" After some discussion, say, "I can stick out my tongue and touch my ear."

Don't give them too much time to think about it before you stick out your tongue and, with your finger, touch your ear.

"Nothing to it."

Death Wish

Here we have a variation of the previous item. This is indeed a death-defying stunt, because afterwards people will want to kill you.

In a discussion of various physical abilities, you might mention that you can wiggle your ears. When challenged, reach up with both hands, grab your ears, and give them a wiggle.

Stand on Your Own Two Hands

When athleticism or agility is discussed, you might mention that you can stand on your hands. "Want to see?"

Whatever they say, stoop down and place your fingers under your shoes. When onlookers scoff, as well they might, you can follow up by asking Roger, "Can you stand on your head?" Spectators will know that you cannot put your head under your shoes, but they might be blind to the other verbal possibility.

So, whatever the answer, say, "Well, I can." Pause. "Just lie down on the floor there."

If they don't get it, continue, "Just lie down there, and I'll stand on your head."

The Trained Flea

"Have you ever seen my trained flea?" you ask Valerie.

She probably hasn't. Pretend to remove a flea from your pocket and set it on your left palm.

After a second, you say to the flea, "Pardon?" Lean your head near your palm so you can hear better. "Oh, he wants to do a few tricks for you. Okay. First, a backflip."

Wave your right finger in a little circle, following the motion of the flea doing its backflip. "Now a double somersault."

Again follow the motion with the first finger of your right hand.

"Terrific." Pause. Then say to the flea, "Pardon?" Lean your head in and listen. "He wants to sit on your palm. Here, hold your hand out."

Hold your hand near Valerie's extended palm. "There he goes! *Nice* jump." To your friend say, "Now don't move your hand too much."

Stare off into space for ten seconds or so. Then turn to the flea and inquire, "Are you almost done eating?"

Pulling the Rug Out

Let us assume that you are a man with a good head of hair or a woman with a fairly short hairstyle. Before we proceed, grab your hair firmly with both hands (Illus. 41). Move your hands forward about an inch and then back. Notice that your scalp is moving. That is the basis of this little stunt.

Illus. 41

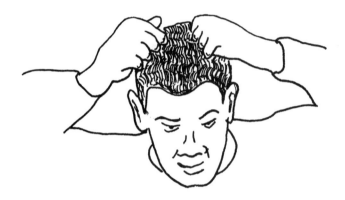

Do this trick when the topic has turned to hair, haircuts, hairstyles, or a kindred subject. I suppose you could bring up the subject yourself. You might say, "I haven't had any trouble with my hair for years. I found the perfect solution long ago."

Grip the back third of your hair, moving your scalp forward, if it is not forward already. Now give a backward tug. Your hair moves quickly backward; the illusion is that you have adjusted your toupee.

"Is it straight?"

You can repeat the tugging procedure a few times.

Practice this in the mirror until the "wig adjustment" looks realistic.

That's Show Biz!

Actor-comedian Art Metrano developed a completely goofy routine, which I have adapted here in part. As he performed the following maneuvers, Metrano would loudly hum, "Everything Is Fine and Dandy." If you choose to try the stunt, I recommend that you either hum that, or something equally peppy.

Start off by holding both hands up. The first two fingers of the right hand are raised. None are raised on the left hand. Move the hands behind your back. Immediately bring them forward with the two fingers of the left hand raised, and none raised on the right hand. As you bring the hands forward, increase the volume of the accompanying music, signifying that something special is happening.

Return to regular volume. Hold both hands up right next to each other. Again, the first two fingers of the right hand are raised. Bounce the two hands together repeatedly. As you do this, quickly lower the first finger of the right hand and raise the first finger of the left hand. Hum louder after you've done this. Return to your regular humming volume.

Still bouncing the hands together, lower the other finger on the right hand, and raise the second finger on the left hand. Hum louder!

Stop. Take a bow.

Commence humming again. Hold up both hands, making an okay sign with thumb and first finger of each hand. The other fingers should be extended. In effect, you're showing two closed rings. Slam the two rings together several times. The last time, briefly separate one thumb and first finger, letting the other ring slide through. Immediately press the thumb and first finger together again. They are now interlocked. Increase the humming volume as you pull the two rings against one another, indicating how securely they are fastened.

Lower the music. Continue pulling the two rings against one

another. Finally, release one ring in the same way as you attached them. In wonderment, note how they are now separated. Increase the volume.

Lower the volume. Reach into your pocket with your right hand and pull out a handkerchief. Stuff it into the left hand, starting at the top. Reach below the left hand and take hold of the other end of the handkerchief. Gradually pull it out into sight. Spread it out and show both sides as you increase the volume of the music.

Return the handkerchief to your right pocket. Remove a coin—say, a quarter—from that same pocket. Display it so that all can see it. Replace it in the same pocket. Show that both hands are empty. With your left hand, reach into your left pocket and remove a quarter. Proudly display it as though you've performed a miracle. The music peaks, and stops.

Take a bow.

I am sure you can invent several additional stunts at least as silly as these.

Notes

(1) I must thank my good friend Jim Smyth, former principal of Southfield-Lathrup High School, who was kind enough to provide from memory (much superior to mine) many of the items in the above routine.

(2) You might decide to use the handkerchief in the interlocking rings routine. Let the handkerchief hang from your mouth by one corner as you display your two rings formed by thumbs and first fingers. Cover the rings with the handkerchief. Pull them out, locked together. Cover them again. Pull them out, separated.

Hanky Panky

As long as you have the handkerchief out, you might as well try some other stunts with it. And, to add some spice to your routines, you might want to include the three items at the end of this chapter that involve paper money.

How Silly Can You Get?

This is not a trick, but it's an entertaining stunt that you can perform for children. At the conclusion of Spooky Spoon (page 31), I presented a version of the same stunt.

Holding a handkerchief in your right hand, grab a corner with your left hand and pull up so that six inches stand straight up in the air (Illus. 42). Note that your right fingers are in front of the handkerchief and your thumb is behind.

Stroke the handkerchief up with the left fingers several times, straightening it, and say: "This is a magic handkerchief. You have probably noticed that one person here is very, very silly. Now, when I wave my hand over the handkerchief and say the magic word—which is 'silly'—the handkerchief will point to the person who . . ."

Illus. 42

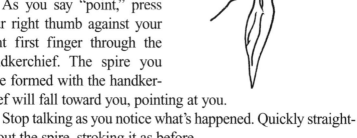

As you say "point," press your right thumb against your right first finger through the handkerchief. The spire you have formed with the handker-chief will fall toward you, pointing at you.

Stop talking as you notice what's happened. Quickly straighten out the spire, stroking it as before.

"As I was saying, someone here is extremely silly. This magic handkerchief will point to that person when I . . ."

Once more, you press your thumb against your first finger, and the handkerchief will point at you. When this happens, you should continue talking for a bit. Children find it quite funny that you're unaware that the handkerchief is pointing at you.

You finally notice that the handkerchief is pointing at you. Now you are getting a bit irritated as you repeat the entire business. Children will find each repetition amusing. Four or five repetitions should be enough. Finally say:

"You know something? This handkerchief is really *dumb*!"

I'm Just Wild About Hair

Twirl a handkerchief between your hands to roll it tight. Now hold it in your right hand, about six inches from the corner, as previously shown in Illus. 42. Note the position of the thumb at the back of the handkerchief.

Pretend to pluck a hair from your head. The invisible hair should be about five inches long. If one this long is not available on your dome, borrow someone else's head. Go through the motions of tying the hair to the very tip of the handkerchief.

Position the hair so that the free end is directly above the handkerchief. Now pull the hair back toward you. Simultaneously push your thumb against the handkerchief and slowly slide the thumb downward, so that the handkerchief slowly bends toward you. It should appear that you are pulling the hand-kerchief back with the hair (Illus. 43).

Illus. 43

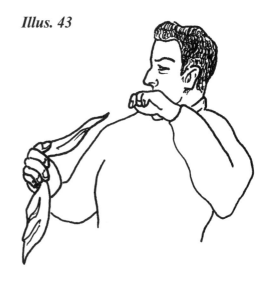

Move the hair forward. The hand-kerchief moves with it as you slowly slide your thumb upward and on top of your first finger (Illus. 44).

Illus. 44

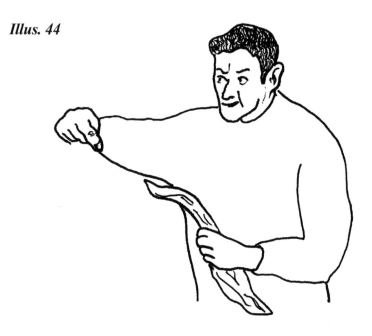

By pressing the thumb to the right and turning the hand slightly to the right, you can cause the handkerchief to bend to the left. But don't bend it too far to the left; you may not be able to bring it straight up again.

Experiment with various moves. It will take some practice to synchronize the movement of the handkerchief with the pulls of the invisible hair, but the reward is a clever stunt you will have forever.

For a climax, you might let the handkerchief hang down as you jerk the hair loose from it. If you happen to be running a bit thin on top, you might lick the end of the hair and try to replace it on your head.

Tie Game

Required: Three handkerchiefs and the ability to tie a knot.

Display two handkerchiefs, one in each hand. Tie them together at one end. Let the two hang from the left hand as you show the third handkerchief in the other hand (Illus. 45).

Pick out an apt young lady—Sherri, for instance—and say to her, "Notice that these two handkerchiefs are tied together. Can you put this third handkerchief between them? You're not allowed to tear them or to untie the knot."

As bright as Sherri is, she will probably have to give up. You may not be as bright as Sherri, but you are much, much slyer.

Tie the third handkerchief to the ends of the other two, so that the three form a triangle. Hold them up so that the third handkerchief is held between your hands (Illus. 46).

Illus. 45

Illus. 46

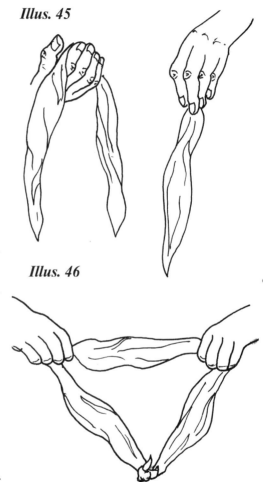

"There you are. I have placed the third handkerchief between the other two."

The Mystic Thumb

Drape the handkerchief over your left hand. Wave your right hand over the handkerchief in magical gestures as a strange phenomenon occurs: Something strange is rising underneath the handkerchief. The handkerchief's surface rises a few inches.

Whip away the handkerchief, revealing that your left thumb was doing the monkey business.

Arrow Dynamic

As long as you have the handkerchief out, you might say, "Now, my impersonation of William Tell."

Hold the handkerchief by opposite corners and twirl it so that it becomes a thin roll. Continue holding it in the same manner as you say, "Here we have my arrow. Over there is my son, with an apple on his head."

Illus. 47

Stretch the handkerchief between your hands (Illus. 47). When you have pulled it taut with the right hand, snap it so that it is propelled to the left. You perform two actions simultaneously: Release the hold of the right hand and make a slight propelling move with the left hand, as though throwing the handkerchief.

The result is that the handkerchief will fly several feet to the left. If you practice a bit, you can get the handkerchief to sail a fair distance.

"Whoops! Missed the apple again. Sorry, son."

A Soft Frisbee

Surely there is some sort of trick we can do with a neatly folded, well-pressed handkerchief. You bet there is. You can spin it out like a Frisbee, and for a considerable distance. You might remove it from your pocket at the beginning of several handkerchief stunts. Toss it to someone on the other side of the room, using the same technique as when throwing a Frisbee. In fact, you might invite the catcher to toss it back. It's *really* not that tough.

Love Knot

Any stunt can be enhanced if you have a little story to go with it. Here's a good example.

This is one of those rare instances where a moment's preparation is necessary. Tie a small square knot in the corner of a handkerchief. Place it in your pocket or purse so that the knot can be readily grasped and concealed when you remove the handkerchief.

Take out the handkerchief with the right hand and hold it so that the knot is hidden by the fingers and the rest of the handkerchief hangs down.

"I want to find out if my boyfriend (husband) *really* loves me. Obviously, the best bet is to use this handkerchief."

With the left hand, pick up the bottom corner of the handkerchief and place it so that it is loosely held in the right hand next to the knotted end.

Snap your right arm downward in the motion you would use in trying to snap a whip. As you do so, release the corner you just placed in your hand. At the same time, say, "He loves me."

Place the bottom corner in your hand again. Repeat the snapping action, saying, "He loves me not."

Do it again, saying, "He loves me."

Snap the handkerchief once more. This time, release the

knotted corner and hang on to the other corner. As you snap, you say, "He loves me not."

Raise your hand so all can see the knot. "Hey, look, I made a knot. A love knot." Pause. "But is it a 'loves me' knot, or a 'loves me not' knot?" Shrug. "I guess I'll never know."

The Utility Handkerchief

Have you ever considered the number of really stupid things you can do with an ordinary pocket handkerchief? Of course not. That's what I'm here for. To entertain your friends, you might whip out your handkerchief and perform some of these:

Illus. 48

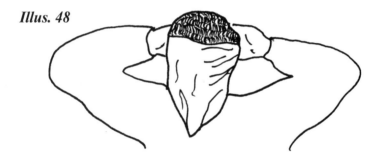

1. *"A stupid hold-up man."* Fold the handkerchief corner to corner and place it high on your forehead, rather than on your lower face (Illus. 48).

Then say, "Stick 'em up!"

2. *"A gypsy."* Still folded corner to corner, the handkerchief goes around your head (Illus. 49).

Illus. 49

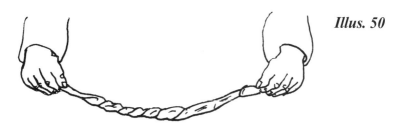

Illus. 50

3. *"A snake."* Holding the ends of the folded handkerchief, twirl it around and around until it becomes long and thin (Illus. 50). Take one end in your left hand, as though holding the snake behind the head. Move it about as you make a hissing sound.

4. *"Or a very large worm."* Hold the ends between your hands again.

5. Tie a knot in the middle of the handkerchief. Ask, "Do you know what that is?" Whatever the answer, say, *"No, that's a knot."*
 Pause.

"Or a snake who has just eaten something."

Illus. 51

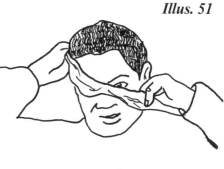

6. Now untie the knot. Stretch the handkerchief diagonally across your face so that it covers one of your eyes (Illus. 51). *"Long John Silver. Arrrr, there!"*

7. Hold the handkerchief up as in Illus. 52. *"A giraffe."* Reverse the position of the hands. "Do you know what *that* is? A giraffe going the other way."

Illus. 52

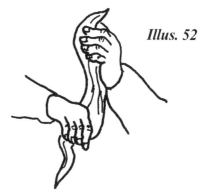

Illus. 53

8. Hold the handkerchief as in Illus. 53. *"Here we have a really skinny elephant."* If everyone looks perplexed, indicate that the trunk is dangling from your left hand, and the tail from your right.
9. Tie the handkerchief into a loose knot. Pull the two ends straight up and hold the handkerchief as in Illus. 54. *"A rabbit."*
10. Fold the hankerchief in half diagonally. Hold one end of the

Illus. 54

Illus. 55

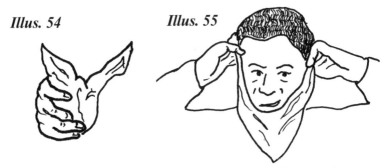

folded handkerchief in each hand. Bring the ends up under your ears and let the handkerchief hang below your lips (Illus. 55). *"Santa Claus."*
11. "And now the thrilling climax." Continue gabbing as you roll the handkerchief up. Hold it just above your head. The thumb and first two fingers of each hand hold the ends of the hand-kerchief; the other fingers press the rolled portion against your thumb (Illus. 56).

Illus. 56

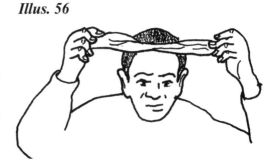

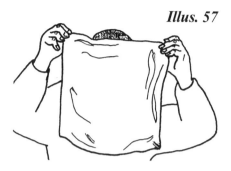

Illus. 57

Say, "Th-that's all, folks!" Release the rolled portion, and the "curtain" comes down, hiding your face (Illus. 57).

The faster you perform these, the better. Incidentally, I am sure you can create several "handkerchief impressions" of your own. As you can see, they need not be clever, just silly.

Silly Bill

A handkerchief can be put to a variety of stupid uses, but so can money. You might whip out a crisp dollar bill and say to your friends, "I wonder if you realize how useful money really is." Then you can demonstrate any or all of the following, performing them as rapidly as possible:

Illus. 58

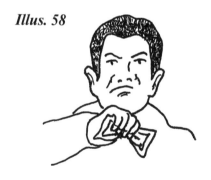

1. Grip the bill on its long sides between your thumb and first finger. Bend the bill inward and hold it up to your neck (Illus. 58). *"A bow tie."*

Illus. 59

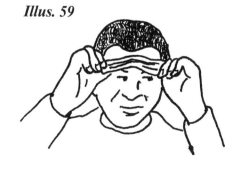

2. Take the bill at either end in your hands and hold it above your eyes (Illus. 59). *"A visor."*
3. Roll the bill up

60

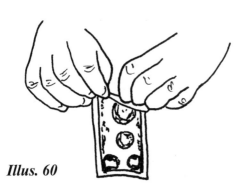

Illus. 60

lengthwise and pretend to sip through it. *"A straw."*

4. Take the rolled-up bill near the top in the same grip you would use to hold a pencil. *"One chopstick."*

5. Starting at one corner, roll the bill diagonally (Illus. 60). "And there's all sorts of useful stuff you can make for Barbie and Ken dolls." Pull an end of the bill so that it telescopes outward (Illus. 61). Hold the small end to your eye, saying, *"A tiny spyglass."*

Illus. 61

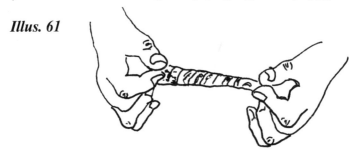

6. Hold the small end to your mouth saying, *"A megaphone."* Then, in a teeny girl's voice: "Give me an S, give me a T, give me a U, give me a P, give me an I, give me a D: Stupid!"

7. Accordion-pleat the bill from one end to the other (Illus. 62).

Illus. 62

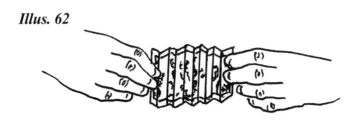

Take it at the ends and move it in and out like an accordion. *"An accordion."* You might sing a bit of "Lady of Spain" in a tiny voice.

Illus. 63

8. Straighten out the bill, fold it in the middle, and place it on the table (Illus. 63). *"A pup tent."*

Illus. 64

9. "And you can do impressions with it." Again, roll the bill up lengthwise. Hold it to one side of your mouth (Illus. 64). *"A walrus with one tusk."*

10. Hold it to your forehead. *"A unicorn."*

11. Place it under your nose and push your lips up (Illus. 65). *"A man with a moustache."*

Illus. 65

Perhaps you can come up with some better ideas. I'm exhausted.

Money Talks

For this stunt, you will need a fairly crisp bill of any denomination. Hold it on its long sides in your right hand between the thumb and second finger (Illus. 66). With your left hand, move the top and bottom inward as you push in the center of the bill slightly with your right first finger. Lift your right first finger away from the bill. Now, move your right second finger toward your right thumb and then release the pressure. Repeat this rapidly several times. The ends of the bill should flap up and down like lips.

Illus. 66

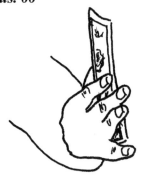

You can now talk to your money . . . and have it answer. Make no attempt to do actual ventriloquism. Simply talk to the money in your natural voice, and use a different voice as the money speaks and you move its lips. What should you and your money talk about? Anything.

Here are some ideas:

YOU: I hear that money talks.

MONEY: That's right, Ace.

YOU: What's your name?

MONEY: Bill. Five-Dollar Bill.

YOU: You look kind of green.

MONEY: Yeah, I don't get out in the sun much.

YOU: Why's that?

MONEY: I live in a dark, shabby wallet. But at least I've got a permanent home.

YOU: You do?

MONEY: Sure, the owner's too cheap to spend me.

YOU: *I'm* the owner.

MONEY: Nice of you to admit it. But at least I'm not lonely in there.

YOU: You're not?

MONEY: No, there are a lot of singles.

YOU: Good.

MONEY: And no bigger Bills to push me around.

No doubt you can work out equally inane things to have your money say to you.

Penny Move

Some time ago, I presented this trick in a book. Since then, I've developed a somewhat simpler method. John Fisher originally developed the stunt; it was improved by Tony Griffith.

Start by placing a small coin—preferably a penny—onto the table. Next to it set six dollar bills in a row.

Dave always appreciates a chance to make some money, so say to him, "Dave, how would you like to make some money?" Sure enough, he wants to.

"Dave, here we have six dollar bills and a penny. You're going to win one of these objects. To do this, you'll move objects around according to a set of rules. As you do, objects will be eliminated. But they'll be eliminated according to decisions that you yourself make. The object that's left is your prize."

Since Dave is starting to look bewildered, explain, "All will be clear in a moment. For right now, please put the six dollars and the penny into a straight row in any order you wish." Set up a possible row so that he gets the idea.

Eileen has a doctorate in philosophy, so she should be able to read the rules to Dave. Ask her if she'll help out, and hand her a copy of the rules.

RULES

1. Make one move.
2. Remove the two end items.

3. Make three moves.
4. Remove the two end items.
5. Make one move.
6. Remove the item on the left.
7. Make one move.
8. Remove the item on the left.
9. Congratulations! You can keep the item that's left.

"In a moment, Eileen, read these rules one at a time to Dave."

Turn to Dave. "Are you sure you want the objects in this order? You can change the order if you wish." When he settles on an order, continue, "I have to tell you what a 'move' is. When you make a move, you exchange the penny with a dollar bill on either side of it. If the penny is on the end, obviously you must exchange it with the bill second from that end. Do you understand?"

He does.

Meanwhile, you've noted whether, as Dave looks at the layout, the coin is at an odd or even position from the left. If it's at an odd position, Dave will end up with it. So you'd tell Eileen to read the instructions one item at a time, and ask Dave to proceed as he wishes.

But if the coin is at an even position from the left, he'll end up with a dollar. In the earlier version, the spectator was given one of two sets of rules, depending on whether the coin was at an odd or even position from the left. I adjusted the working so that you could always use the "odd" rules. That is, when the coin was lying at an even position, you moved it to an odd position before the reading of the rules. Here's how:

You have just finished explaining what a "move" is. And you have noted that the penny is in an even position. Say to Dave, "Just to make sure we both have the same idea, would you make a move for me, Dave." He makes a move. "Excellent! Now let's proceed."

The coin is now at an odd position. When Dave follows the directions, he'll end up with it.

Somewhat Hypnotic

Let's return to something that resembles real magic. I'm referring to a number of stunts that depend on fake hypnotism.

I really don't know much about hypnotism. I know enough about stage hypnotism, however, to be extremely skeptical about all hypnotism. Undoubtedly, a great many persons do believe in hypnotism. This means that you and I have a wonderful opportunity to pretend that we can hypnotize people. This alone might not be entertaining. But the stunts presented here will certainly fascinate any group.

How do you present hypnotism? Clearly, however you wish. You may decide to make a serious presentation in which you stare hypnotically, make mysterious gestures, and speak in smooth, hypnotic tones.

Or, you may take a more cavalier attitude, pretending you can perform "instant hypnotism." "All I need to do is gesture, and you're in my power. Why, I can hypnotize better than Mandrake the Magician . . . and without the help of a big bodyguard to make sure people stay hypnotized."

Or you might try my approach: "Let's try some experiments in hypnotism. I'm not sure if they'll work, but I have high hopes. It's especially possible if we use suitable subjects. Let's see. We might try . . ."

Whatever approach you take, you'll find these stunts extremely helpful.

Incidentally, most of these stunts work because of little-known physical limitations. Some are just plain sneaky. The first one is a case in point.

We Will Join Together

This is the first of four stunts that *seem* to involve tests of strength, but in fact do not. A fairly strong man is the best subject for this first stunt, so let's try Spike. Ask him to stand up and place his two fists one on top of the other (Illus. 67). He is to extend his arms and try to hold his fists together.

Illus. 67

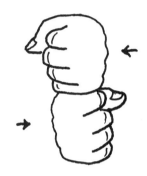

With the first fingers of each hand, you sharply tap the backs of Spike's hands in opposite directions, as indicated by the arrows in the illustration. He will find it impossible to hold his fists together.

After a few tries, he may want to see if you can do it. If not, you might say, "Would you like to try it on me?"

Extend your two hands just as Spike did, only with the top hand secretly grip the thumb of the other hand. From the front, it looks perfectly normal. He will not be able to tap your fists apart.

You may wish to amuse the group by revealing what a sneak you are. Otherwise, quickly drop your hands and separate them so that no one can see what you did.

He Has No Pull

Here's another apparent test of strength. Since Fred fancies himself a powerful man, let's test his strength.

Hold up the first fingers of both hands. "I have two peculiar fingers," you explain. Wag one finger. "This one is positive." Wag the other. "And this one is negative. When I press the two

Illus. 68

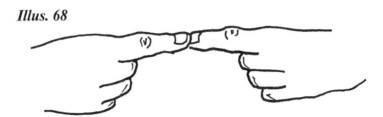

together . . ." Do so. ". . . it is almost impossible to separate them" (Illus. 68).

Grimace as you try to pull the fingers apart, with no success. Address Fred: "You're a strong man." He agrees. "How about seeing if you can pull my fingers apart. But I have a rule: You can only grip my arms above the elbows."

As Fred grips your arms, press your two fingers together with all your might. The leverage is all wrong for poor Fred. No matter how strong he is or how he grasps your arms, he will have a terrible time trying to separate your fingers. Unless he is extraordinarily powerful, he will not succeed. Lesser mortals will find it totally impossible.

To make it extremely difficult, you might suggest that Fred try to perform the feat as he stands behind you.

He Exercises Weakly

Let's try that again, with a slightly different spin.

Arnold is very proud of his powerful physique, so he'd be the perfect subject for this experiment. Myra also agrees to help out.

"Myra, I'd like you to touch your forefingers together at about shoulder level, and close to your body."

Gesture hypnotically at Arnold. "Sorry, Arnold, but that gesture eliminated some of your enormous strength. Now I'd like you to grasp Myra firmly at the wrists. And, Myra, I'd like you to push your fingers together as hard as you can. Arnold, don't squeeze too hard; we don't want you to hurt Myra. But I'd like you to try to pull her hands apart. Just pull steadily; no fair giving a big jerk—nothing personal. Ready? Go!"

Chances are, Arnold won't be able to separate her hands. And if he does, it will be with some difficulty, which will also serve the purpose.

Don't wait too long before you say something like this: "Your strength is returning, Arnold. Myra, you're getting weaker, weaker. Arnold, you're getting stronger. Myra, you can hardly hold your fingers together."

Continue like this until Arnold separates her hands.

Using Your Head

Finally, you might as well make a few hypnotic motions and take Arnold's strength away again. Then place your hand flat on the top of your head and press down hard (Illus. 69).

"Arnold, try to remove my hand from the top of my head."

Illus. 69

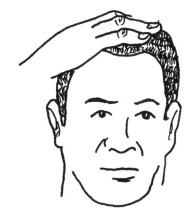

He tries and tries, but cannot. You gesture with your other hand, returning his strength to him. Now he can lift your hand, mainly because you make no effort to keep your hand on top of your head.

Just a Touch

Let's try a stunt that's been around for many decades, perhaps more than a century. The subject should be a fairly light man—Glen, for example. He sits in a chair.

You get four others to help out. Have two of them place their first finger under his armpit. Two others place their first fingers under his knee.

Tell the four, "You're to lift Glen up. After you've raised him a foot or so, put him back down."

Tell the four to *lift*. Chances are nothing will happen. For one thing, there was no coordination. Explain this.

Tell the four helpers that you'll count to three, and then they should all lift together. At the count of *one*, Glen should blow out, getting rid of all his air. At the count of *two*, they should all draw a deep breath.

Count to *three*, deliberately and clearly. If all goes well, Glen should be raised into the air. If it doesn't go well, forget it. Again, it was probably a lack of coordination. Move on to something that's bound to work.

Strong Arm

Yet another test of strength, and this the sneakiest by far. Mike and Bruno have lifted weights for years. For some odd reason, they think they are stronger than you are. It's high time you called their bluff.

Hold a glass of water in your right hand. Ask Mike and Bruno to grip your right arm in any way they wish. They may use both hands, and they may hold your arm as firmly as they wish.

"Hold my arm as tightly as possible," you conclude, "it will make no difference. I will be able to raise the glass to my mouth and take a sip."

Once they get their grip, ask if they are ready. They are. You, of course, take the glass in your left hand, raise it to your lips, and take a sip.

For Shame!

Place your hand palm down on the table, with the fingers extended and pressing against the table. Now fold under your middle finger so that the joint farthest from the fingernail is also pressed against the table (Illus. 70). Retaining this position, you will be able to move your thumb, your first finger, and your pinky. But you will be unable to move your third or ring finger.

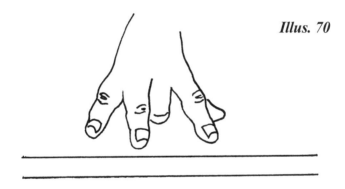

Illus. 70

Can something amusing be made of this? Oh, yeah.

Larry has always proven himself to be true blue, so he'd be the perfect sap for this stunt. Have him extend his hand on the table with his middle finger folded under. "You must retain this position with your finger tucked under while you try to answer my questions. All right?"

Propose the following actions, leaving appropriate pauses so he can try each task.

"Are you an honest person? If so, lift your thumb. All right, put it back."

"Do you have a sense of humor? If so, lift your first finger. All right, put it back."

"Are you loyal to your girlfriend? If so, lift your little finger. All right, put it back."

"Are your answers truthful? If so, lift your ring finger." Pause. "I said, 'If so, lift your ring finger.' Well, I guess that tells us something."

Here's a slightly different possibility.

Let's work with Elaine, who is engaged to Bill, also present. Have her place her left hand on the table in the position described above. (You may have to demonstrate.)

"Elaine, when your hand is pressed to the table like that, it can reveal certain secrets about your forthcoming marriage. For instance, try to lift your thumb, while keeping everything else pressed down."

She lifts her thumb.

"Ah, that indicates that throughout your marriage, you will have Bill under your thumb. Now lift your first finger." Point to the appropriate digit. She lifts it.

"That's your pointing finger. When you're married, anything you point to, Bill will get for you—jewelry, furs, cars. Now lift your little finger." She does so.

"Any time you wiggle your little finger, Bill will leap to perform your orders. Now lift your ring finger." Point to the digit. Of course she cannot lift it. "Are you trying your hardest?" She is.

"Most peculiar. I think it means this: Now that Bill knows all that other stuff, he's going to run away before the wedding. Sorry about that."

You can work your patter according to the situation. For example, if Lois cannot move her ring finger, it means that she *will* marry Ron, a man she is not fond of (and who is not present).

Going Up!

Leon will probably be a good subject.

Explain to him, "Through some mysterious power, Leon, I'm going to force you to raise your arm, no matter how hard you try not to."

Have him extend his right arm straight out from the shoulder, palm up. "Now I'll work on raising your arm, perhaps just a little. Meanwhile, you try to hold your arm steady."

Make a hypnotic gesture or two if you wish. Then begin to stroke the top of his extended hand very rapidly and gently. As you do so, press downward. Repeat the move at least ten times.

Perform the move a final time, except this time you don't touch his hand. Instead, you pass your hand an inch or less above his palm and quickly withdraw.

If all goes well, in anticipation of your stroke, Leon will involuntarily push up.

Still Going Up!

Later, with Ted, you might try a similar stunt.

Say, "Ted, please hold your hands out, palms up." He does so. "Now I'm going to stroke your palms, and I'd like you to do what you can to keep your hands from being forced down. If I have the power, something very unusual may happen."

With the tips of your fingers, stroke his palms toward you several times. Take your hands away. Repeat the procedure, taking your hands away again. Now place your hands over Ted's as though you're going to begin again, but don't touch his palms. Rather, continue the stroking motion as you slowly lift your hands.

As a rule, Ted's hands will rise, following your hands.

Nod. "I told you."

Crank It Up

Let's try one of the more perplexing and amusing stunts.

Doris hasn't been hypnotized lately, so let's subject her to one of our mesmerizing spells.

"Doris, I'd like you to interlock your fingers (Illus. 71)." She does. "Next, please extend your elbows out to the side." Again, she obliges.

Illus. 71

"Now I'd like you to push your palms together as hard as you can. The idea is to pretend someone is trying to separate your hands and you won't permit it."

For at least ten seconds, encourage her to keep pushing hard.

"You can stop now, Doris. Please raise your first fingers and hold them so that they're about an inch apart." Show her with your own fingers (Illus. 72).

Illus. 72

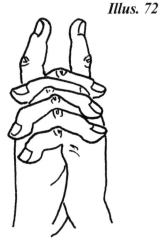

Move your right hand next to Doris's extended first fingers and make a small circling movement, as though you're turning a small crank. At the same time, make whatever you think will pass for a cranking noise.

As you make this move, Doris's first fingers will slowly move together and touch. It's a most peculiar phenomenon to see.

Strong Will

If Doris seemed quite receptive with the previous stunt, she'll probably be perfect for this one, which is similar in effect.

"Please clasp your hands, Doris, intertwining your fingers. Just as you did before, extend your first fingers up so that they're about an inch apart. Now point your hands downward, please."

The reason for the latter instruction is that you don't want her looking at her hands and exerting conscious control of her first fingers.

"I'll try to force your first fingers together. Let's see if I can do it."

With your fists, push with all your might from either side of her clasped hands. *But don't actually make contact with the hands.* Doris's first fingers gradually move together and touch.

But sometimes not. In which case, you congratulate her on her strong willpower and proceed to another stunt.

Stick 'Em Up

Peter would be perfect for this stunt, which is based on a principle similar to that used in Crank It Up.

"Peter, please stand in the doorway and push the backs of your hands against the frame. Pretend you're afraid that the frame might collapse and you're trying to prevent that with the backs of your hands."

He stands in the doorway. "Please stay there for a count of 50."

Either he or you count to 50 aloud.

"Please drop your arms to your sides, Peter, and step forward." He does.

You make an upward motion with your arms. Sure enough, Peter's arms rise slightly from his sides. In some instances, his arms will rise several inches. Occasionally, the rise will be almost imperceptible.

A Real Side-Kick
• • • • • • • • • • • • • • • • • • • •

Announce in a grandiose manner that you are psychic. "Not only that," you continue, "but I can hypnotize anyone else and make that person psychic."

Certainly there will be skeptics, but you should be able to get a volunteer. Assume Agnes is foolish enough to step forward. Wave your hands hypnotically in front of her eyes. "Soon you will be under my spell," you say, "and then you will be every bit as psychic as I am. Do you feel the power?"

Whatever she responds, say, "I know that you now have the power." Hold up a folded piece of paper. "Do you know what I have written on this paper?"

"No."

Open the paper and show that indeed Agnes is psychic, for you have printed NO on the paper in bold letters.

"See? You knew, you knew!"

Suppose your psychic friend does not answer no; suppose she says, "Uh-uh," or shakes her head. Say, "What?" Keep saying it until you get your correct response. Eventually you should. If you don't, ask someone else, "What is she trying to say?" You will probably get an emphatic, "She's trying to say no!"

Wanna Bet?

Let's try some challenges using the hands.
Some of these are magical (the first one,
for instance) and some are puzzling.
All are intriguing. There is no need to keep any
of these secret. Some, by their very nature,
can't be kept secret; you must explain how they
work or there's no point. Others are very
deceptive, so failing to explain them is somewhat
unfair. As far as I'm concerned, the point to
most of these is: "Don't play the other person's
game." The other person is very likely
to know something that you don't. In other
words, I believe that such stunts should be
instructive, perhaps even educational.

Knock It Down
• • • • • • • • • • • • • • • • • •

Agnes is always bragging about her keen eyesight. Now's the time to foil her.

Stand a small object on a table. It could be a cork, the cap of a ballpoint pen, whatever. Have Agnes stand back about ten feet from the table.

"Agnes, please hold out your right hand with the first finger extended. Then take about four steps toward the table. *Immediately* reach out and knock over the (object) with your first finger."

Chances are excellent that she'll miss on the first try.

Hippety Hop
• • • • • • • • • • • • •

The "do-as-I-do" stunt is always very popular. Those who catch on feel very smug, and those who don't are extremely curious. All are entertained.

"I wonder if any of you can do 'hippety hop' exactly the way that I do it. First, I'll show you. Then, you can try."

Hold up your left hand, palm toward yourself. With your right first finger, touch, in order: the tip of your thumb, your first finger, second finger, third finger, fourth finger, third finger, second finger, first finger, thumb. That is to say, you proceed from your thumb to your little finger, and back again. As you touch each digit, say a word: "Hippety hippety hippety hop. Hippety hippety hop. Hippety hop." Lean back and fold your arms.

In other words, say, "Hippety hippety hippety hop (You are now on the third finger). Hippety hippety hop (You have touched the fourth, third, and second fingers). Hippety hop (you are back to the thumb)." Afterwards, lean back and fold your arms.

Let others try. If they miss a step, repeat the action. Most will omit the tricky part *at the end* . . . when you fold your arms.

Ahem

• • • • • • •

Place any two small objects on the table or on the floor, about eight inches apart. "I challenge anyone here to do exactly what I do," you declare. "If by some stroke of luck you *do* figure it out, please keep the secret so that others have a chance to get equally lucky."

Cover the object on the left with your left hand and the object on your right with your right hand, saying, "I can do this . . ." Cross your hands, covering the opposite objects, and say, ". . . but I can't do that."

Let other people try. They will probably fail. Congratulate anyone who succeeds. Repeat the action, and let others try it. By the time you have done it four or five times, at least some of the group should catch on.

What you do each time is *clear your throat with a slight cough* and then cover the objects with your hands and make your declaration. Before long, others will clear their throats before beginning. Ultimately, each person will begin the action with extremely loud hacking. Loads of fun for all. Except, perhaps, for those who take a long time catching on, or who never get it at all.

A Dollar Down

• • • • • • • • • • • • • • • •

Sometimes this simple little stunt can entertain for as long as five minutes.

Tricia's fingers may just dance over those piano keys, but let's find out how quick her reactions really are. Show her a dollar bill, telling her, "I'll bet you can't grab this dollar when I drop it."

Demonstrate how she is to hold her hand, and then hold the bill by one narrow end, letting it hang down. Hold it directly above her hand so that it will fall between her fingers (Illus. 73). Tell Tricia, "When I drop the bill, you grab it. But remember:

Illus. 73

This is a test, this is only a test. If you catch the bill, you don't get to keep it."

You're just kidding, however. Her chances of catching the bill are slim to none. Nor will repeated tries improve her chances.

In a group, just about everyone will want to give it a try. But resist the temptation to try it yourself; you won't be any more successful than anyone else.

You must actually try this ancient stunt out to see how effective it is.

A Hand-Me-Down

With your right hand, pick up an object—a book, for instance. Raise your extended arm to the side, until you're holding the object at shoulder level. Raise your left arm the same way (Illus. 74).

Illus. 74

Regina is staring curiously, so you address her. "Regina, can you hold the book like this and then transfer it to your other hand? You can't bend your arms or bring them toward each other."

Hand her the book. If Regina works it out, she deserves your congratulations. Otherwise, you show her how: Keeping your arms in the same relative position, bend down and set the book on a table. Turn around, bend down, and pick up the book with the other hand.

How Touching

Steve seems awfully sure about almost everything. Propose this to him: "Steve, with your assistance, I believe that I can put your left hand where your right hand can't touch it."

If he has trouble understanding, repeat the proposition. He finally accepts your challenge.

Take his left hand and cup his right elbow with it.

Give It Some Thought

Time to give Sylvester something to think about.

Hold out your right arm and bend your wrist toward your elbow. Make several bending movements. Still holding out your arm, say, "Huh! I wonder. Say, Sylvester, can you touch your elbow with your hand?"

He may actually try. Finally, he must say, "No."

"I can," you declare proudly.

Touch your right elbow with your left hand.

Give It *More* Thought

If Sylvester isn't tired of playing the sap, you might try this one.

"If you'll let me, Sylvester, I think I can put something on your left hand that you can't pick up with your right hand."

He thinks not.

Dip your hand into a glass of water, and let a drop fall onto his hand.

Give It *Lots* of Thought

"Time for a test, folks."

Hold out your left hand with its back toward the group. Fold in your thumb so that only the extended fingers are on display. Carefully adjust them back and forth.

Finally ask, "Which two fingers are farthest apart?"

Let them guess for a few moments. Then say, "I believe that it's these two."

With your other hand, touch the fourth finger and the first finger.

The Coin Clutch

Andy thinks he can do just about anything. It's time someone taught him a lesson. Tell him, "Under certain conditions, I'll place a coin between two of your fingers, and you won't be able to let go of it."

Have him place the knuckles of his right hand against those of his left. Then he is to extend his third (ring) fingers and hold the tips together. You slide a coin between the tips of the two extended fingers.

"Hold your knuckles together and try to release the coin." It is quite impossible.

Hey, Don't Push!

This can be performed any time, under any circumstances.

Indicate an object on the table, such as a glass or a bottle. "See this bottle?" Connect your left thumb and first finger in the "okay sign," and display it. (See Illus. 32 in Now *Really* Listen!) "I'll bet I can push it through this hole."

Surely someone will think such a deed is impossible.

Poke your right first finger through the hole and push it against the bottle. "See? I told you I'd push the bottle through the hole."

He Just Can't Wait

Is Harvey really *that* gullible? Now's the time to find out.

"Harvey, I have a proposition for you. You crawl under the table. I'll knock on top of the table three times, like this." Knock three times. "That's the kind of knock I'll make. Now, I won't do anything whatsoever to you. Still, I'll bet that you come out from under the table before I knock the third time."

Let's say that he, or someone even more gullible, takes you up on it. He crawls under the table.

"Are you ready, Harvey?"

He sure is.

Knock on the table twice and then stop.

Eventually, he'll come out. Most people have no desire to spend the balance of their life crouched under a table. After Harvey finally emerges, you might give the third knock.

The Dramatic Duo

If a deck of cards is handy, you can perform an astonishing trick that requires no more than your ability to speak.

Pick up the deck and glance through it, studying the faces. Turn it face down and give it a shuffle.

"That should take care of it."

Turn to Bruce. "Name two values, Bruce. For example, you might name king and four—whatever you wish."

He names two values.

"I'd be willing to bet that they're together in the deck. Let's check."

Fan through the deck so that all can see. Sure enough, you'll find the two values together. If not, they might be separated by one card. When that happens, say "Whoops, I missed it by one."

Regardless of the outcome, perform the stunt at least once more. Fan through the cards face up. Give the deck a shuffle, and then announce that you're ready.

What's the trick? There is no trick. Any two values will probably be together in the deck. That's all there is to it.

Impressions

*What could be more entertaining
than a flock of off-beat impressions?
Lots of things, of course.
But these are all impromptu,
and feature hands and feet.
So, to perform them, you need
nothing but a good memory.*

Beat That Egg

An old-fashioned eggbeater.

Move one arm around and around as your knees move in and out in a waddling movement.

That's a Lot of Tap Shoes

A tap-dancing alligator.

Stretch out face-down on the floor. Bend your arms at the elbow, while your feet are straight out. Move your hands and feet up and down as you hum "Tea for Two."

Walk a Little Slower

A guy trying to steal shoes at a department store.

Put your feet close together. Move one forward a few inches; move the other a few inches in front of it. Continue like this, giving the impression that the shoes are tied together.

The Crawl of the Wild

A caterpillar crawling up a tree.

Without bending over, move your hands down as low as you can. Thumbs and first fingers are together, forming an arch.
(1) Move your left thumb up to press upward against the left first finger.
(2) Raise your left first finger into the air.
(3) Move your right thumb up to press upward against the right first finger.

(4) Raise your right first finger so that it presses its tip against the left first fingertip, forming the original arch once more.
(5) Repeat the entire sequence.
(6) As you move along, keep raising your arms slightly, indicating the ascent of the caterpillar.

Poor Little Plane

A lost airplane.

Hold your arms out as you make the sound of an airplane in flight. Look from side to side. Your expression gets more and more bewildered. Gradually, you change from the airplane sound to the sound of crying.

Very Sharp

A pencil sharpener.

Stick your left first finger into your left ear (not far, *please*). Do a winding motion with your right hand by your right ear.

Stop winding and pull the left finger out of your ear. Look at the end. Not done yet. Reinsert it and begin winding again. At last, stop winding. Take the left finger from your ear. Inspect the end. Nod your head. Blow on it.

Squeaky Clean

One man taking a shower.

Hold up the first finger of your left hand, the back of the hand toward the group. Hold the right hand palm down above it. Move the fingers rapidly back and forth.

The More, The Merrier

Five men taking a shower.

Hold up the left hand with its back to the group. Extend four fingers. The thumb is folded in.

Once more, hold the right hand above the left, moving the fingers back and forth.

Someone is bound to observe, "That's not five; that's only four."

Turn your hand around, showing the thumb.

Say, "One guy's washing his feet."

If no one comments that it's not five guys, you say, "Wait, that's only four guys. Oh, yes, one guy's washing his feet."

Little Things Mean a Lot

A little person playing the piano.

Get down on your knees. Reach out well above your head with both hands and pantomime playing on the keys.

The Animal in Us

One elephant.

Throw a suit jacket over your head, letting one sleeve dangle down. Move your head back and forth.

Two elephants.

The same jacket over the same head. Let both sleeves dangle as you move your head.

I Salute You

Presenting a variety of salutes.

A paratrooper.

Salute and bring your hand away in front of your head. Extend your fingers and thumb, simulating a parachute, as you gradually lower the hand.

A short soldier.

Salute about a foot above your head.

An overweight soldier.

Bring your arm up to salute, but stop about a foot short.

Siamese twin soldiers.

Salute with both hands.

A female recruit with long fingernails.

Salute, leaving nails stuck to the head. Go, "Aghhh!" With difficulty, use your other hand to pull the hand loose.

A Little Push

A tube of toothpaste.

Stand facing the front. Put your hands at your side in the arms akimbo position. Push in. Move the hands away slightly and then push in again. Do it once more. This time, in response to the push, stick your tongue out.

Fore . . . Heaven's Sake

Me golfing.

A bit of acting is required. Pretend to hold a golf club as you take your stance. Look at the ball. Waggle the club several times. Take a mighty swing.

Smile as you look straight down the fairway. Less confidently, slowly look from side to side. Finally, look down at your ball, which is still there.

Hit the club against the ground as you say quietly, "Oh, darn!"

Number, Please

The number four.

Lift up your right leg and place the foot against your left knee. This forms a fairly decent number four.

You might add, "I can also do the number one."

Straighten up and stand there rigidly, hands at your side.

Take a Guess

Back in the mid-thirties and up through the fifties, there was a popular pursuit in which a person would perform some sort of absurd action and then ask what it represented. In other words, these are pretty much the exact opposite of the impressions in the previous category. In most instances, the result of these impressions was considerable amusement. Here we have some of the better ones, primarily using the hands. The majority of the items are from Martin Gardner's exhaustive book, Encyclopedia of Impromptu Magic.

Excuse Me!

Move your hand randomly through the air. From time to time, snap your fingers and jerk your hand in another direction.

Take a Guess:

A butterfly with the hiccups.

Ride Down?

Hold up a fist, with the back of your hand to the group. Your thumb is hidden from the group. Move your hand from side to side several times.

Take a Guess:

A thumbless guy hitchhiking.

Mirror, Mirror

Put the fingertips of one hand against the fingertips of the other. Move the palms in and out as you gradually raise them.

Take a Guess:

A spider climbing up a mirror.

Come Fly with Me

Wave your arms up and down as though flying.

Take a Guess:

A man painting a narrow hallway.

Present Arms

How about some items
that mainly deal with arms?
Good! I thought you'd
like that idea.

Put On Your Coat

This looks really silly. You can do it at the beginning of a performance, or at the end. As a matter of fact, you can casually perform it for friends; just make sure you have their full attention first.

Let the left sleeve of your coat or jacket slide off your arm. With your right arm, swing the coat low behind your back, and to the front.

Stick your left arm back in the sleeve. Swing the coat back over your head, and push your left arm back in all the way. This should be done rapidly and smoothly.

But chances are quite good that you will mess up your hair.

Relax and Unwind

How about a good, old-fashioned arm stretch? I thought that would interest you.

You must be wearing a coat or jacket. Lose part of your left hand in the sleeve. Then hold the left arm parallel to the floor, pressed across your body.

Grasp the tips of your left fingers with your right hand. Give repeated tugs, pulling the hand little by little out of the sleeve. The sleeve retains its position because it is pressed firmly against the body.

With each tug, make a little clockwise movement with the right hand and make a vocal grating sound, as though gradually unwinding the hand.

After you have moved the hand out as far as possible, reverse the motions, gradually moving it back.

A Good Choke

Many people are familiar with the routine where you stand in a doorway with your arms extended out of sight. Then you appear to be strangled as you reach back and take yourself by the throat.

There is more to be done with this position, however.

Stand in the appropriate position, your arms out of sight.

Pretend to address an unseen stranger: "Please get out of my way."

Pause. "What? Why should I get out of *your* way? I was here first."

Pause. "What do you mean you were here first? Get out of my way before I do something I'll be sorry for."

Move your head forward. With your right hand, reach out and slap your cheek.

"Of all the nerve!"

Bring your right arm into sight. "I'll show you!"

Reach out and slap your left hand. "How do you like that?"

Your right arm is out of sight again. Slap yourself in the face again. Slap the invisible opponent again.

Now the invisible opponent reaches out and begins choking you, as you open your mouth and go, "Aghhhh!"

He lets go, and you walk away.

A Good Backup

This is old but good. The impromptu nature of this favorite always keeps it fresh.

One example: You are to sing a song. Your friend stands behind you. Your arms go behind your back. Your friend's arms are extended under your armpits. As you sing, your friend does the gestures. He can do all sorts of goofy things to you—wipe your face, scratch your nose, clean your ear, gesture extravagantly at the wrong parts of the song, and so on.

More extravagant presentations are possible. You can prepare a recipe, for example, or put on makeup.

Double-Jointed

Put on a pair of gloves or mittens. The one on your right hand goes on normally. The one on your left hand goes on upside down. In other words, this glove goes on so that your thumb goes into the little finger of the glove, and your little finger goes into the thumb of the glove.

Stretch your arms out and place your hands on the table, palms down. The fingers of your right hand bend down; the fingers of the left hand bend up. It appears that your left hand is incredibly twisted.

Showtime

It's time for you to stop fooling around with removing fingers, stretching them, doing impressions, and other silly stunts.
Now take center stage and perform entertaining hand routines that are really magic.

A Pat on the Head

Surely you remember this one. The trick is to rub your stomach with one hand while patting the top of your head with the other. Just about anyone can manage it after a few tries. The trick is to reverse the procedure, without changing the hands. In other words, you must immediately switch to patting your stomach and rubbing your head.

It's more difficult than you think.

You can provide considerable entertainment at friendly gatherings by getting everyone to give it a try.

"Ladies and gentlemen, may I suggest that we attempt a test of coordination. This is precisely the same test given by the Air Force to prospective pilots." One little lie—big deal! "The object is to rub your stomach and at the same time pat the top of your head with the other hand. Like this . . ." Demonstrate.

"The hard part, however, is to leave the hands as they are, but switch their motions. In other words, start *patting* your stomach, and *rubbing* your head. Let's start by patting our heads and rubbing our stomachs. Go!"

When everyone seems to be doing well, call out, "Switch!" Most will have trouble making an immediate switch. As soon as everyone succeeds, call "Switch!" again. Just keep on switching until the well runs dry.

Some people just cannot seem to get the knack. They are not particularly embarrassed since the feat itself is so useless and ridiculous.

I like to lead by performing the actions myself. Despite my advantage of considerable practice, I occasionally err, which enhances the enjoyment of others.

It's Superman!

"Call me a glutton for punishment, call me a crazy guy; here's what I'm going to do. Before your very eyes, I am now going to perform between three and four hundred push-ups."

(If you are not athletically inclined, you may choose to make that sit-ups instead of push-ups.)

Drop to the floor and perform five push-ups. Jump to your feet and take a bow. "I was happy to do it for you. That's right—five push-ups. That's between three . . ." Hold up three fingers. ". . . and four hundred."

Mime Time 1

It's time to present several items that will require considerable rehearsal. All of these are old standards that, done properly, always provide considerable enjoyment—both for the performer and the observers. So select a few and work on them until you have the movements and the timing down perfectly. It will be well worth your while. And you'll be extremely pleased when you receive requests for particular items.

Illus. 75

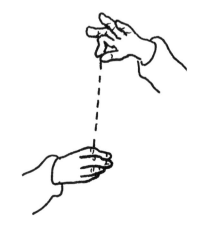

The first one is pretty easy.

Pretend to pull a hair about 12 inches long from your head. If you don't have long hair, pretend to take a hair from a better-equipped friend. You might say, "Let me borrow a strand of hair; I'm running a little short."

Hold the hair directly in front of you, as if it is hanging from your left hand. Run your right finger and thumb from top

Illus. 76

Illus. 77

to bottom of the presumed hair (Illus. 75). When you reach the bottom, give the hair a jerk, straightening it out. Repeat the move.

With your right first finger, smack the hair at the bottom so that it swings to the left. Presumably, the hair is now swinging back and forth like a pendulum. As it goes to the left, follow it with your eyes without moving your head (Illus. 76). In the same way, follow it with your eyes as it goes to the right (Illus. 77). Follow the back and forth motion several times.

Finally, take the hair and, holding it at each end between the hands, return it to the head of the person who loaned it to you. Or, perhaps, smooth it onto your own head.

Mime Time 2

Let's get a bit more complicated.

Take a piece of make-believe thread from your pocket. Untangle it; then move your right hand away from your left as though drawing it along the length of the thread. Make the distance between the hands about two feet. Let go of the end held by your right hand, which now takes the left end from the left hand.

Now the thread is hang-ing from your right hand, and your left hand is free. With your left hand, remove an invisible needle that is stuck in your jacket, sweater, shirt, or blouse. Hold the needle up, point between your left thumb and first finger. Lick the end of the thread and insert it through the eye of the needle (Illus. 78). Draw the thread through the eye so that the length of thread is doubled, with the right hand holding both ends of the thread. Let go of the needle and let it hang down as you tie the two ends together in a knot.

Take the needle in your right hand and smooth out the length of thread with the left. Bring the point of the presumed needle above your right eye. Push the needle through the upper eyelid and then the lower eyelid. Bring your right hand about a foot below your right eye, presumably still holding the needle. Jerk your hand down a half-inch or so and, at the same time, wink. Repeat the wink several times.

No need to put the material away. You'll need it for the next stunt.

Mime Time 3

Thread an imaginary needle exactly as in the previous stunt, tying a knot in the end. As before, the original invisible thread should be about two feet long.

Hold up your left hand. Separate your little finger from the other digits. Push the needle through the side of the finger. On the other side of the finger, grasp the needle and, with an upward

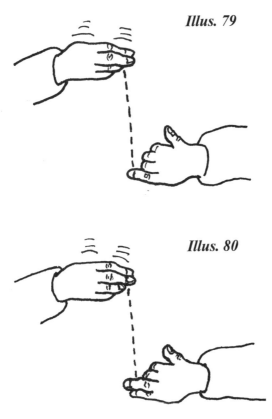

Illus. 79

Illus. 80

sewing move-ment, pull all the thread through (Illus. 79). Give a little jerk with the right hand; simul-taneously jerk the left hand up a bit, as though you moved it with the thread, through the little finger.

Come back with the needle and push it through the third finger of the left hand. Take the needle and pull it upward again. As you near the top of your upward sweep, bring the little finger up so that it is next to the third finger (Illus. 80). Again give a little jerk with the right hand, simultaneously jerk-ing the left hand slightly.

Sew the other two fingers in the same way, so that all four fingers are sewn together. Hold your hand with your palm toward spectators as you swing the thread over the forearm so that you are holding the needle to the rear of the left hand.

Pull down on the needle, lowering all four fingers (Illus. 81). Raise the needle, and the left fingers return to their original posi-tion (Illus. 82).

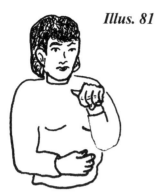

Illus. 81

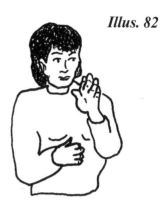

Illus. 82

Repeat the pulling/raising movement several times, causing your left hand to wave bye-bye.

Wrap the thread around the needle and put the little packet away.

Mime Time 4

Crook your right first finger (Illus. 83). Place it near the outer edge of your right eye and pull down slightly.

"Hey, lady, can't you hang your umbrella somewhere else?"

Illus. 83

Take away your right first finger. Crook your left first finger. Place it at the outer edge of your left eye and pull down slightly.

"Gosh, thanks, lady."

A Touching Experience

At a party, you might declare, "I feel the presence of a ghost in this house. Anyone else have that feeling?"

Millie probably has the same feeling, so say to her, "Good. Maybe we can demonstrate that the ghost is actually here."

You face each other, sides to the group, and as far away from the group as possible. "I'd like to try a test to see if you *really* feel the presence of the ghost. Everyone else has to promise not to try any funny business, okay?"

The group agrees.

Say to Millie, "As you know, ghosts don't particularly like to be seen, so I will need you to close your eyes. Not yet! You'll want to know where my hands are at all times, so I'll use them to help you keep your eyes closed. Stand very still, please."

Bring your hands up, first fingers extended toward Millie. Slowly move your hands toward her eyes. When you're an inch or two away, she will close her eyes. When she does, place the first and second fingers of one hand on her eyelids, pressing *very, very gently.*

"If there *is* a ghost around, I'd like to speak to it. Oh, ghost, please make your presence felt." Pause. "Good heavens! I see a vague figure floating above us."

Flick her hair with the fingers of your free hand. Ask her, "Did you feel it?"

You can quickly perform other ghostly deeds, like tapping her wrist, snapping your fingers near her ear, or placing something on her head.

You might take out your keys, for instance, saying, "Hey, put that back! It's got my keys." Then place the keys onto her head.

After several quick stunts, extend the first finger of your free hand and move the hand just in front of her eye. Withdraw the two fingers from her eyes, instantly folding in your second finger, so that you're back to the original position. As you remove your fingers from her eyes, say, "You can open your eyes now."

After making sure Millie has a good look at your hands, drop them to your sides.

"Whoops! The ghost is gone."

Usually, while the ghost is manifesting itself the group will join in, indicating that they can see the ghost. In all likelihood, the only problem you'll have is convincing your subject that no one else in the group participated.

Occasionally, your subject will pull away, opening her eyes. Quickly drop both hands to your sides and look as innocent as you possibly can.

Creepy Caterpillar

It happens that you have an ugly little creature in your pocket. "Have you ever heard of a transparent caterpillar?"

Probably not.

"It happens that I have one here." Remove the invisible caterpillar from your pocket, placing it on the palm of your left hand. "He's extremely well-trained. Watch him now. He's going to creep all the way around my hand. Ready, set, go! Look at him go! He's almost at the side of my hand." Pause. "Wow! He's started underneath. That little rascal is creeping right along." Hold up your hand so you can see him crawling underneath. "Look at that, he's almost at the other side." Pause. "Now he's starting up the side toward the—whoops! His hat fell off."

Lean down and pick up an invisible small hat from the floor. Address Diana: "Hold this for me, will you?" Hold the hat out; she will undoubtedly take it in her hand.

You look back at your palm. "Look at that! He's right back in the center of my palm. I think he set a personal speed record." Pause thoughtfully. Address Diana: "You think I'm crazy, don't you?"

"Yes."

"Well, how about you? You're the one who's holding his hat."

If she should answer no, say, "Oh, yes you do. But you're as bad as I am. After all, you're holding his hat."

And the Beat Goes On

Waving your arm up and down spasmodically, snap your fingers in a totally random beat. After about ten seconds of this, continue snapping as you sing out, "I've got rhythm, I've got rhythm."

Finger Folly

Let's say you address Leona: "I've been having trouble with my fingers lately." Shake your head. "How many fingers have *you* got?"

"Ten," she will respond in the tone usually reserved for morons other than yourself.

"Do you mind folding your hands so I can count them?"

Show her what you mean by clasping your hands as in Illus.

Illus. 84

84. When Leona does so, slowly and carefully count her fingers. "That's right. Ten."

"Now count mine for me, will you?"

You fold your hands and extend them toward Leona. She counts your fingers, and comes up with nine.

"Doggone it," you say, "that's what I thought." Drop your hands to your side. "Oh, well. Nine's my lucky number."

How did you do it? You simply tucked your left second finger into the palm of the right hand and filled that space in appropriately with the other fingers. (In Magnetic Spoon 2, page 27, you'll find that Illus. 23 shows the key positions.)

And One Left Over

This could be a snappy follow-up to Finger Folly. "I wish I could figure out what's wrong with these fingers. Look."

With your right first finger, count the fingers on your left hand, starting with your thumb. "One, two, three, four, five." Continue the count with your left first finger, starting with the little finger of the right hand. "Six, seven, eight, nine, ten. So far so good. But look at this."

With the first finger of your left hand, count backwards, starting with your right thumb. "Ten, nine, eight, seven, six."

Hold up the fingers of your left hand. "And five is eleven."

Pause. "It gets very confusing."

Miraculous Multiplication

This is a stunt, all right, but it's far from crazy. In fact, it's quite clever. Elementary school students may even find it useful. More important, it is entertaining.

Young Jim is always willing to learn something clever, so tell him, "Are you aware that you carry a handy-dandy calculator with you everywhere you go? Well, you do—right on your fingers. Any time you wish, you can do the most difficult of all the multiplication tables on your fingers . . . instantly. I'm referring, of course, to the multiples of nine. Quick! What's nine times eight?" Instantly continue: "I thought so. You need this."

Have Jim hold both hands up, palms toward him. "Now we'll number your fingers from left to right as you look at them."

Point to the left thumb. "This is number one."

Point to the left first finger. "This is two."

Continue with the other fingers of the left hand. Then point to the little finger of the right hand. "This is six."

Complete that hand, ending with the thumb as ten or zero. The numbering is shown in Illus. 85.

"Now you want to do nine times something. What do you choose?"

Let us say he chooses four.

"Very well. Nine times four. Lower finger number four." If he has trouble with this, bend his number four finger down so that the hands look like Illus. 86.

Illus. 85

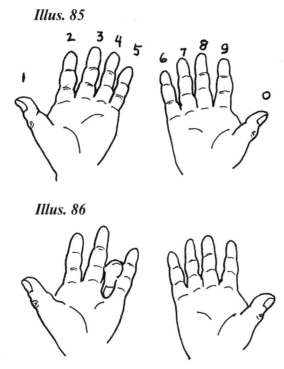

Illus. 86

"There is a space now among your fingers. There are three fingers on the left side of the space. That means your first number is three. There are six fingers on the right side of the space. That means your second number is six. Three, six. Nine times four is thirty-six.

"Let's try nine times eight. Lower finger number eight." He does so. "There are seven fingers to the left of the space, so your first number is seven. There are two fingers to the right of the space, so your second number is two. Seven, two. Nine times eight is seventy-two."

The right thumb is ten when you multiply and zero when you look at the result. The only time it matters, of course, is when you do nine times ten, which is fairly easy anyway, even for the mathematically illiterate.

Note

If the child is fairly good at math, you might explain an even easier method. When figuring multiples of nine, consider the number that you're multiplying nine by. Suppose, for example, that you're doing 3 times 9. Subtract 1 from the number 3, getting 2. Subtract 2 from 9, getting 7. The digits are 2 and 7 . . . or 27.

Suppose you're multiplying by 5. The first digit will be 4 (one less than 5). Subtract 4 from 9, getting 5—the second digit. The answer: 45.

Let's try 8. Subtract 1 and you get 7—the first digit. Subtract 7 from 9 and you get 2—the second digit. The answer: 72.

Snatch and Grab It

Make a fist with your right hand, and stick the thumb straight up (Illus. 87). Enclose the fist with your left hand (Illus. 88). (The protruding right thumb should be at the approximate point where your left thumb would be when extended.)

Quickly pull the right hand down and try to grab the formerly protruding thumb. Naturally, it doesn't work.

Assume the position again. Give it another try. Again, you fail. And you're getting a little irritated.

You get even angrier when you miss for the third time.

Illus. 87

Illus. 88

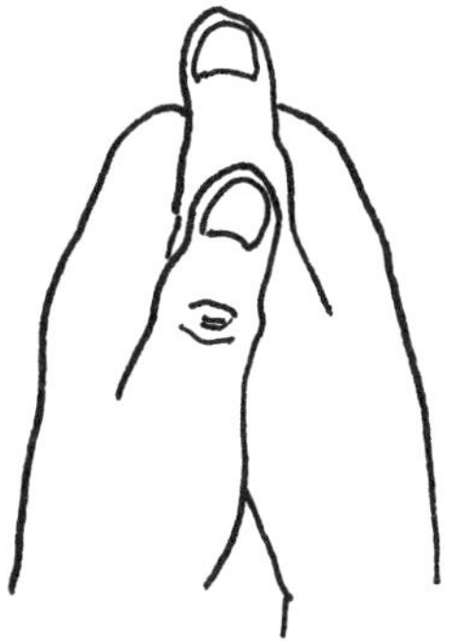

This time when you bring your right hand up to be enclosed by the left, keep your thumb down. Instead, stick your *left* thumb up.

Now when you grab for the thumb, you get it!

Get a good hold on it, shouting, "Hey, I finally got it!"

Shake your hand several times. Then release your grip, showing the left thumb. Give a "thumbs up" gesture with it, and then proceed to another stunt.

Dead Digit

A small box is needed for this venerable trick. The perfect choice used to be a small matchbox, but it's not nearly so available nowadays. With a bit of cutting, though, you can use the box containing ink for the printer, or a lightbulb container, or a box that contained staples, and so on.

Cut a hole in the bottom of the box. Insert your middle finger so that it seems to rest in the box.

Put some cotton around your finger. (You can get some from an aspirin bottle or other pill container.) Put some red coloring on the finger where it meets the nail. (This is supposed to be blood, but is not completely necessary.)

Put some talcum or other powder on the finger. It should look pretty gruesome by the time you put the top on the box.

How do you use this setup? You might approach Grace, saying, "Look what I found."

Lift back the top of the box.

She will undoubtedly be horrified at the sight of the finger. Let her enjoy it for a moment or two, and then wiggle the finger a little. Her enjoyment will undoubtedly be multiplied.

Note

This is truly an antediluvian trick. But just as a great old joke is still funny to those who haven't heard it, so is this completely appalling to the unsuspecting.

Maneuvers

As yet, we haven't really
investigated some of the maneuvers
possible with the hands.
Here we have several that are
calculated to interest observers.
Although no special skill is required,
a bit of practice may be necessary.

Greetings Gate, Let's Coordinate

Let's start with an amusing one that's a bit more difficult than it appears—at least in some of the variations.

This is best done seated, though it can be done standing. Your right hand grips your nose, and your left hand grips your earlobe. Let go. Both hands come down and slap your knees. Then your *left* hand grips the nose, and your *right* hand grips the earlobe. In the original version, the hand grips the earlobe that's on the same side as the hand.

In a variation, the hand always grips the *same* earlobe. Or to make it more complicated, you can vary it: Do two turns where you grip the earlobe that's on the same side as the hand, and then do two gripping the same earlobe. To further complicate things, you can follow up by doing two turns gripping the opposite earlobe.

Finally, you can do variations with the hands hitting opposite knees.

Clearly, performing all the deviations requires considerable rehearsal.

Climbing Up!

"I've been studying the techniques of firemen and of great mountain climbers, and now I can climb *anything* with extraordinary speed. I'll demonstrate how fast I can go."

Hold your hands at about stomach level. With the right first finger, touch the pad of the left thumb. Retaining contact, turn the right hand clockwise, and the left counterclockwise, revolving the finger on the left thumb and bringing the right thumb up to the left first finger.

Next, revolve the right hand counterclockwise and the left clockwise, as you bring the right first finger up to the left thumb—the starting position. Repeat these movements extremely rapidly. As you do, raise the hands bit by bit until your arms are extended to full length over your head.

Drop your hands, exhaling sharply. "I'm exhausted."

Honk, Honk

This maneuver was a favorite of that hilarious silent Marx brother, Harpo. He would swing his arm around as though his elbow were a rubber band. You, too, can perform this feat, but it will require a bit of practice in front of a mirror.

To get the correct starting position, you should hold your left arm out to your left, so that it is shoulder high. Now bend it at the elbow, forming a right angle, the fingers pointing at the floor. The back of the hand is toward the audience.

Ready? With the right hand, grasp the left fingers and pull them to the right several inches. Release the left fingers. Make the left forearm go back and forth like a pendulum. Do this a few times.

The next portion, when practiced and done properly, creates the illusion that the left arm can bend in an absolutely impossible way. As described above, your upper left arm is extended from the shoulder and the left forearm is at a right angle to it, with fingers pointing down. With your right hand, grasp the left hand as before. Pull it to the right a bit and then give it a little push to the left.

The forearm pivots in a complete clockwise circle, returns to its original position, and then swings back and forth in gradually smaller arcs.

How do you do it? At one point in the circle, the left arm is extended straight out. At this point, turn your left hand palm outward. The hand continues around 180 degrees and is somewhere near your chin. At this point, turn your left hand palm inward again. The whole circular movement must be quite rapid, and the revolving arm must be kept on a *flat plane*.

The illusion is quite startling. It's probably best not to do a repeat until another occasion.

I Got Rhythm

You can produce an excellent rhythm following this procedure:

Place the left hand, palm down, onto the table. Smack the back of it with the right hand. Roll the left hand over away from the right hand, smacking its back against the table. Roll the left hand back. Smack the back of the left hand with the right hand.

Moving the hands fairly rapidly, the rhythm is produced like this:

Smack the back of the left hand with the right hand (*SOUND ONE*).

Roll the left hand over, hitting the table with it (*SOUND TWO*).

Roll the left hand back, hitting the table with the palm (*SOUND THREE*).

Smack the back of the left hand with the right hand (*SOUND FOUR*).

A neat little sound feast is created like this:

Perform the above procedure twice. Then do the first three sounds twice. Finally, do all four sounds.

The rhythm goes like this (back of the hand slaps are in italics):

da-da-da-*da*
da-da-da-*da*
da-da-da
da-da-da
da-da-da-*da*

I'm sure you can work out other interesting rhythms for yourself.

Finger Wiggle

This maneuver is quite useful. When doing a card trick, for instance, you can perform it over the deck before producing the selected card. Or, you can present it as a weird finger exercise.

Put your hands together as though praying. Bend both middle fingers down, the finger on the right hand going on the far side of the other. Now turn the hands so that the right hand is palm-down and the left hand is palm-up. The middle fingers are sticking out of each side. This is accomplished by moving the right hand counterclockwise and the left hand clockwise; meanwhile, both middle fingers remain extended.

Holding the hands parallel to the floor, move both middle fingers back and forth several times, as though they are connected.

Let's Coordinate

Here we have an example of excellent coordination. Others who see you perform this will have some difficulty duplicating it.

Start by placing your right first finger on top of the fleshy portion of the left thumb. Retaining the position of the right first finger, turn the right hand clockwise until the right thumb touches the fleshy tip of the left first finger.

The right thumb retains its position on the left first finger as you proceed with the next move. Pivot the right hand counterclockwise until the right first finger returns to its original position on the tip of the left thumb.

Repeat this move several times.

You're now ready to advance. The next time when you pivot the right hand clockwise, the thumb lands on the tip of the left second finger. The counterclockwise pivot returns the right first finger to its original position on the left thumb.

Repeat, going to the third finger, and then the fourth finger.

To make it more interesting, work it backwards, going from the left fourth finger back to the first finger.

Have you mastered it? Good. Now let's make it really tough.

Touch the left first finger to the tip of the right thumb. Now work your way through the right hand exactly as you did with the left.

Tough Workout

"It's time for a little exercise," you declare. "I've been taking it easy long enough."

Hold your hands out about twelve inches apart, fingers pointing up. Close up the second, third, and fourth fingers, leaving the first fingers sticking up.

Fold up the first fingers so that they still extend slightly above the other fingers. Raise the first fingers again. Fold them up again.

Once more, extend the first fingers, but as you do, bend the hands so that they turn toward each other. The extended first fingers are pointing at each other, about an inch apart. Return the hands to the original position and, at the same time, fold in the first fingers.

Raise the first fingers up. Fold them down. Point the first fingers at one another. Return to the starting position.

Keep repeating this again and again. It really looks peculiar.

Finally stop, declaring, "Whew! I'm exhausted."

Magical Feet

*Hands, hands, hands! That's hardly
fair to those other extremities.
How about feet? Surely, they deserve
some attention. Right. So, here we
have a number of foot tricks —
some magical, some just plain stupid.*

Take a Walk

Standing behind a couch, you announce: "A man walking down-stairs."

Starting at one end of the couch, you walk to the other side, taking small steps. As you move along, you bend your knees more and more, lowering yourself. Practice a bit; the illusion is most droll.

But Seriously, Folks

"I can do a perfect imitation of a man going upstairs."

Just stand there, facing the group.

Eventually, someone (if not everyone) will say the equivalent of, "Well?"

"Pardon? Oh, you see, I'm on an escalator."

Or an elevator.

Take a Stand

Ask Rudolph to stand against the wall sideways, his one foot against the wall.

"Now, Rudolph, please lift your other foot."

He'll find it quite impossible. You can make a big show of it.

"Come on, Rudolph, don't be so stubborn. Just lift your foot. After all, it wouldn't hurt for you to cooperate."

Too bad. He just can't do it.

Dancing Fool

When attention is focused on you, perform a brief tap dance in which you clomp your feet as clumsily as possible. Climax it by clapping your hands and extending your arms toward the group. At the same time, sing out in your best Gene Kelly manner, "Gotta dance!"

It's Underfoot

It's time to pull a prank on Hope, who is far too clever for her own good.

"I have been trying to perfect a little experiment," you explain. "I wonder if you'd help me out."

Hand the suspicious thing a pencil and paper. "I'll turn away, and you write any three words you want on the paper. Remember, just three words. And I will tell you what's on the paper without even glancing at it."

Turn your back while she writes. "Now fold the paper twice, place it on the floor, and stand on it."

Turn back, saying, "I am now ready to tell you exactly what is on that paper." Concentrate fiercely. "Your foot . . . is on that paper. Thank you so much."

If Hope tells you that your experiment is stupid, you might say, "I'll admit it needs a little work."

Towel Trick 1

For the next three tricks, you'll need a large colorful towel. A beach towel would be perfect. In all three tricks, your shoes should be quite loose; in fact, before you start, you might slip your feet out of the backs of the shoes.

"Ladies and gentlemen, a fabulous disappearance!"

Hold the towel in front of you so that it hangs down to your shoes. Bend one leg back at the knee, leaving the shoe on the floor. Raise the towel a foot or so (Illus. 89). Apparently, one leg has disappeared.

Illus. 89

Move the towel back down.

"And now, yet another miracle!"

Do the same trick with the other leg.

Towel Trick 2

Continuing your performance, move to the far right end of the towel. Let the towel hang all the way to the floor. Slip off your shoes and stand behind them. Raise the towel slightly so that all can see your shoes. Make sure the rest of the towel hangs to the floor.

Slide a few feet to the left, getting on your tiptoes. This should create the illusion that you're floating away from your feet. Lower yourself and return to your shoes.

Towel Trick 3

Carrying on, you have moved back to your shoes. Stand in them and move back to the middle of the towel. Hold the towel so that the bottom rests on your shoes. Gradually lower yourself (and the towel).

"The incredible shrinking man!"

Make sure the shoes do not get covered by the towel; instead, it should sort of bunch on top of them. Kneel on your shoes.

Shuffle around a bit, moving slightly from side to side.

"The incredible *growing* man!"

Gradually stand up. Get your feet into your shoes the best you can, and then whip the towel aside.

"Thank you so much."

Take a bow. Point to the towel. Move the top portion forward, as though it's taking a bow. It doesn't matter whether there is applause. In fact, if there isn't, you can take advantage by saying such things as, "Please, please, hold it down; others are trying to sleep. No, no, I really don't deserve it."

The Big Jump

"I can put three chairs together, take off my shoes, and jump over them."

"No you can't."

Put three chairs together. Take off your shoes. And then jump over your shoes. Oh, you daredevil!

Mastery Levels Chart & Index

Trick	Page	Easy	Harder	Advanced
Ahem	79	★		
And the Beat Goes On	106	★		
And One Left Over	107	★		
Animal in Us, The	88	★		
Are You Still Listening?	38	★		
Arrow Dynamic	54	★		
Bad Habit	38		★	
Beat That Egg	86	★		
Big Jump, The	121	★		
"Broken" Finger, The	20	★		
But Seriously, Folks	118	★		
Climbing Up!	112	★		
Coin Clutch, The	82	★		
Come Fly with Me	92	★		
Come and Go	23		★	
Confidentially, It Shrinks	18			★
Crank It Up	74		★	
Crawl of the Wild, The	86		★	

Trick	Page	Easy	Harder	Advanced
Creepy Caterpillar	105	★		
Dancing Fool	119	★		
Dead Digit	110		★	
Death Wish	44	★		
"Dig It" Digit, The	10		★	
Dollar Down, A	79	★		
Double-Jointed	96	★		
Dramatic Duo	84	★		
Excuse Me!	92	★		
Eye Test	40	★		
Farewell Finger, The	39		★	
Finger Folly	106		★	
Finger Stretch 1	15		★	
Finger Stretch 2	16			★
Finger Wiggle	115			★
Floppy Fingers	19	★		
Fore . . . Heaven's Sake	90	★		
For Shame!	71	★		
Funny Farewell Finger, The	39	★		
Give It *Lots* of Thought	82	★		
Give It *More* Thought	82	★		
Give It Some Thought	81	★		
Going Up!	73	★		
Good Backup, A	96		★	
Good Choke, A	95			★
Greetings Gate, Let's Coordinate	112		★	
Hand-Fed	43	★		
Hand-Me-Down, A	80	★		
He Exercises Weakly	68	★		

Trick	Page	Easy	Harder	Advanced
He Has No Pull	67	★		
He Just Can't Wait	83	★		
Hey, Don't Push!	83	★		
Hippety Hop	78		★	
Honk, Honk	113			★
Hot Stuff	42	★		
How Silly Can You Get?	50		★	
How Touching	81	★		
I Got Rhythm	114			★
I'm Just Wild About Hair	51		★	
Impossible Revolution	22			★
I Said, "Listen!"	36	★		
I Salute You	89	★		
It's Superman	99	★		
It's Underfoot	119	★		
I Want to Be Hoppy	25	★		
Just a Touch	70		★	
Kiss on the Hand, A	41	★		
Knock It Down	78	★		
Let's Coordinate	115			★
Listen!	36	★		
Little Push, A	89	★		
Little Things Mean a Lot	88	★		
Loose Thumb	34			★
Love Knot	55		★	
Magic Touch, The	44	★		
Magnetic Spoon 1	26	★		
Magnetic Spoon 2	27	★		
Mentalic	31	★		
Mime Time 1	99	★		

Trick	Page	Easy	Harder	Advanced
Mime Time 2	100			★
Mime Time 3	101			★
Mime Time 4	103	★		
Miraculous Multiplication	107		★	
Mirror, Mirror	92	★		
Money Talks	62		★	
More, the Merrier, The	88	★		
Mystic Thumb, The	54	★		
Now *Really* Listen!	37	★		
Number, Please	90	★		
Pat on the Head, A	98		★	
Penny Move	63		★	
Poor Little Plane	87	★		
Pulling the Rug Out	46		★	
Put On Your Coat	94		★	
Real Side-Kick, A	76	★		
Relax and Unwind	94		★	
Ride Down?	92	★		
'Round and 'Round She Goes	21		★	
Rubbery Pencil	29		★	
Silly Bill	59	★		
Snatch and Grab It	109		★	
Soft Frisbee, A	55		★	
Spoiled Spoon	29		★	
Spooky Spoon	31	★		
Squeaky Clean	87	★		
Stand on Your Own Two Hands	44	★		
Stick 'Em Up!	75	★		
Still Going Up!	73		★	
Strong Arm	70	★		

Trick	Page	Easy	Harder	Advanced
Strong Will	75	★		
Take a Stand	118	★		
Take a Walk	118	★		
That's a Lot of Tap Shoes	86	★		
That's Show Biz!	47	★		
Thumb Stretch 1	12		★	
Thumb Stretch 2	14			★
Thumb to Nose	40		★	
Tie Game	53	★		
Touching Experience, A	104		★	
Tough Guess	39	★		
Tough Workout	116		★	
Towel Trick 1	120		★	
Towel Trick 2	120		★	
Towel Trick 3	121		★	
Trained Flea, The	45	★		
Using Your Head	69	★		
Utility Handkerchief, The	56	★		
Very Sharp	87	★		
Walk a Little Slower	86	★		
We Will Join Together	67		★	
Wrong Number	43	★		

Books by Bob Longe

Card Tricks Galore
Clever Card Tricks for the Hopelessly Clumsy
Clever Close-Up Magic
Easy Card Magic
Easy Card Tricks
Great Card Tricks
The Jumbo Book of Card Tricks and Games
The Little Giant Book of Card Tricks
The Little Giant Book of Magic Tricks
The Little Giant Encyclopedia of Magic
Magic Math Book
Mind Reading Magic Tricks
Money Magic Tricks
Mystifying Card Tricks
Nutty Challenges & Zany Dares
101 Amazing Card Tricks
World's Best Card Tricks
World's Best Coin Tricks
World's Greatest Card Tricks